MᶜCOOK COLLEGE

THE MILITARY HALF

*An Account of Destruction in
Quang Ngai and Quang Tin*

The Military Half

An Account of Destruction in Quang Ngai and Quang Tin

JONATHAN SCHELL

VINTAGE BOOKS
A Division of Random House
NEW YORK

I OFFER THIS BOOK with love to my brother
Orville, who, against everyone's better judgment,
suddenly dropped out of his junior year in college
to set out for the Far East as third cook—
or vegetable peeler—on a Norwegian
dynamite freighter,
and thus set the basic style for the
many impulsive, unlikely trips East
we have both made since.

I WOULD LIKE TO EXPRESS my gratitude
to Ngo Long, who gave me great help
in preparing some
sections of this book, and shared
with me his
amazingly thorough and deep
knowledge of his country
and its people.

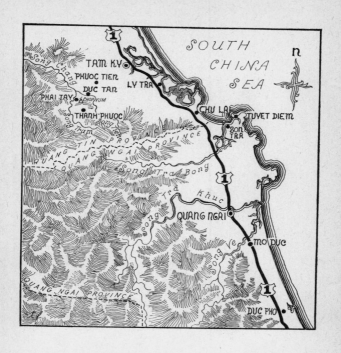

The Military Half

This book is about what is happening to South Vietnam—to the people and the land—as a result of the American military presence. I shall not discuss the moral ramifications of that presence. I shall simply try to set down what I saw and heard first-hand during several weeks I spent with our armed forces in South Vietnam last summer. What I saw and heard had to do mostly with the destruction that was going on in South Vietnam, but at the same time I found that the peculiar character of this war tended to be defined for me by how the men in our armed forces reacted to the various special conditions of the war: the immense disparity in size and power between the two adversaries, the fact that Americans are fighting ten thousand miles from home, the fact that the Vietnamese are an Asian and non-industrialized people, the fact that we are bombing North Vietnam but the North Vietnamese are incapable of bombing the United States, the fact that our bombing in South Vietnam can be met only by small-arms fire, the fact that it is often impossible for our men to distinguish between the enemy and friendly or neutral civilians, the anomalousness and the corruption of the Saigon government, the secondary role played by the South Vietnamese Army we are supposedly assisting, the fact that the enemy is fighting a guerrilla war while we are fighting a mechanized war, and, finally, the overriding, fantastic fact that we are destroying, seemingly by inadvertence, the very country we are supposedly protecting. Like many Americans, I am opposed to the American policy in Vietnam. As I came to know the American men who were fighting there, I could feel only sorrow at what they were asked to do and what they did. On the other hand, I could not forget that these men, for the most part, thought they were doing their duty and thought they had no choice, and I could not forget, either, that they were living under terrible stress and, like fighting men in any war, were trying to stay alive and hold on to their sanity. If our country stumbled into this war by mistake, the mistake was not theirs. If our continuing escalation of the war is wrong, the guilt is surely not theirs alone. If one disaster after another is visited upon the Vietnamese people, these disasters are the inevitable consequence of our intervention in the war, rather than of any extraordinary misconduct on the part of our troops. Thousands of Americans, of course, have lost their lives or been wounded in Vietnam, many of them in the belief that they were fighting for a just cause, and some of the men I came to know in Vietnam will lose their lives or be wounded in that same belief. Some of our men have been brutalized by the war, just as I might have been brutalized if I had been fighting beside them, and just as men on both sides of all wars have been brutalized. Yet some of them have done the job assigned to them without losing their compassion for the noncombatant Vietnamese, or even for the enemy in combat. In this article, however, I am not writing, essentially, about the men in our armed forces. I am writing about a certain, limited segment of the war—about the destruction by the American forces, as I observed it (mostly from the air), of a particular rural area of South Vietnam. All of us must share the responsibility for this war, and not only the men who bear arms. I have no wish to pass judgment on the individual Americans fighting in Vietnam. I wish merely to record what I witnessed, in the hope that it will help us all to understand better what we are doing.

In the spring of 1967, the United States Military Assistance Command in South Vietnam formed a new force, called Task Force Oregon, by assembling the 196th Light Infantry Brigade, the 3rd Brigade of the 4th Infantry Division, and the 1st Brigade of the 101st Airborne Division in Quang Ngai Province, which is the fifth province south of the Demilitarized Zone along the coast of the South China Sea. The creation of Task Force Oregon, which was to operate under the command of the 3rd Marine Amphibious Force, freed elements of the 3rd Marine Amphibious Force, which had been conducting operations in Quang Ngai since May of 1965, to move north to help combat increased activity along the Demilitarized Zone. The Annamese mountain range swings close to the sea in Quang Ngai Province, and between the mountains and the sea is a strip of arable flatland eighty kilometres long, twenty-five kilometres across at its widest point, and ten kilometres across at its narrowest point. The Allied Forces divided this strip, which supports more than eighty per cent of the province's population, of approximately six hundred and fifty thousand, into four Tactical Areas of Responsibility, of roughly equal size, and assigned one each, from north to south, to the 196th Light Brigade, to a brigade of Korean Marines that had landed in Quang Ngai in the summer of 1966, to a brigade of the Army of the Republic of Vietnam (abbreviated as ARVN and pronounced "Arvin" by the Ameri-

5

cans), and to the 3rd Brigade of the 4th Division. The 1st Brigade of the 101st Airborne Division was reserved as a roving force that could be flown anywhere in the province by helicopter to launch surprise attacks on enemy units. The principal mission of the troops that formed Task Force Oregon was to find and kill soldiers belonging to what are called main-force units of the Vietcong (or V.C., or National Liberation Front) and to the Army of North Vietnam who were operating in Quang Ngai Province. In order to break up any fixed patterns of operation that might help the enemy to predict their movements, elements of Task Force Oregon sometimes went outside Quang Ngai, carrying their operations into Quang Tin Province and Binh Dinh Province, which are adjacent to Quang Ngai on the north and on the south.

Task Force Oregon's area of operation was part of a mountainous coastal region of South Vietnam that stretches south from the city of Hué to Binh Dinh Province, and had traditionally been known for its natural beauty and its poor, proud, and hospitable people. Because even the narrow strip of flatland that lay between the mountains and the coast in this region was too sandy for good crops, a large proportion of the villagers long ago took up other occupations, such as fishing in the South China Sea and lumbering in the mountains. Many took up home crafts, and the area became famous for silk and for mats woven of reeds that grew on the banks of the local rivers. Predominantly a rural people, the natives of these mountainous provinces spoke with a broad, flat accent that had a simple, country ring to the ears of a Vietnamese from Saigon. They were also reputed to be shorter than most other Vietnamese, and to have plain, clear features, square jaws, and bold, frank natures. As late as 1964, most of the primary schools in the area adorned their walls with the traditional Vietnamese motto "Though your clothes may be soiled, keep your honor unspotted." Perhaps because the land was too poor to provide an adequate base for large fortunes, wealthy people in these provinces were particularly conscientious about giving their children the best education possible. Before the country was partitioned in 1954, the academic standards in most parts of what is now South Vietnam were far below the standards in the North, but students from the mountainous coastal provinces were noted for giving an excellent account of themselves at Hanoi University, which was regarded as the best in the country at that time. A large number of Vietnam's most popular writers were born in the region, including the late novelist Nhat Linh, who attacked the colonial French and corrupt Vietnamese officials in novels of social protest, and later became a hero to young people in Saigon when he led a movement of scholars and students against the regime of President Diem. The mountainous inland regions of the northern provinces were populated by primitive tribes known to the French as Montagnards, who lived by burning away patches of the forest, cultivating the cleared land until the soil was exhausted, and then moving on to another site.

Historically, the people of the region were rebellious and aggressive. It was from the provinces of Quang Ngai and Binh Dinh that the rulers of the Nguyen dynasty, in the sixteenth century, launched their long drive southward; when the French began their subjugation of Vietnam, in the late nineteenth century, it was in Quang Ngai and Binh Dinh that armed resistance to French rule was strongest; and it was in these provinces, again, that peasant rebellions first broke out, in the nineteen-thirties, against Vietnamese officials who served the French. After the Second World War, when the Vietminh, the anti-colonial predecessor of the National Liberation Front, launched the revolutionary campaign that eventually expelled the French from Vietnam, Quang Ngai became a principal center of revolutionary activity, and French troops never succeeded in entering the province in force. In 1948, for purposes of fighting the revolution, Ho Chi Minh divided the nation into military zones of four types, which he called "free zones," "guerrilla bases," "guerrilla zones," and "occupied zones," and he designated the provinces of Binh Dinh, Quang Ngai, and Quang Nam (north of Quang Tin) as free zones, meaning that those areas were to be considered already freed from the French and from the Emperor Bao Dai. The town of Duc Pho, in the southern part of Quang Ngai Province, became one of the largest rest centers in the country for Vietminh soldiers. The women of Duc Pho had always been famous for their beauty and their fiery, independent spirit, and there was a ditty that warned the "fighting man" who came to Duc Pho to be faithful to his jealous Duc Pho girl friend or risk losing his manhood at the girl friend's hands. In 1954, when many of the Vietminh soldiers and political organizers withdrew to the North, enough of them stayed behind in Quang Ngai and the provinces adjacent to it to insure that the influence of the government in Saigon would not penetrate beyond a few of the region's larger towns. By the early nineteen-sixties, a whole generation of young people in rural areas had known no government other than that of the Vietminh and the National Liberation Front. Not only had they learned to read and write in Vietminh and National Liberation Front schools but they had also learned to sing revolutionary songs, accompanying themselves on the guitar or mandolin, in the course of a drive by the Front to teach young people to play musical instruments. In early 1962, because these provinces were known to be National Liberation Front strongholds, the government in Saigon launched its Strategic Hamlet Program with particular vigor there. The program was intended to separate the people from the Front soldiers and organizers who lived among them, and as a means of accomplishing this the government ordinarily forced the people to leave their villages and to construct fortifications and new habitations at another site. Under a *corvée* system it had devised, it made each man responsible for constructing a certain yardage of wall around the strategic hamlet. If a family refused to move to a strategic hamlet, troops of the South Vietnamese Army might burn its home and its fields; by the end of 1962 parts of Quang Ngai—particularly areas near the mountains—were dotted with the ruins of burned houses. In Quang Ngai, as in other parts of the country, this program aroused hostility toward the government in Saigon, and within two years it was abandoned, to be reconstituted later as the New Life Hamlet Program. Usually, when the government succeeded in constructing a strategic hamlet, the Front quickly reëstablished—or simply maintained—contact with the villagers at their new site, and, consequently, in almost every case the strategic hamlets themselves were under the control of the Front. Supporters of the Front often wrote mottoes on the gates and walls of the strategic hamlets. One inscription, a couplet from the classical Chinese, appeared with particular frequency. It read, "How long can the Great Wall stand/When its base is not the heart of the people?"

At the end of August, 1967, after four months of military operations, Task Force Oregon announced that it had killed, and counted the bodies of, thirty-three hundred enemy soldiers, had "detained" five thousand people, and had captured eight hundred firearms in caches or on or near the dead. It also announced that two hundred and eighty-five Americans had been killed and fourteen hundred wounded. During that August, I travelled as widely as I could in Quang Ngai Province, in order to talk with military people and civilians, and to observe what the effect of the Allied military operations had been, and I also observed several of the military operations themselves, as they were being carried out by Task Force Oregon in the northern part of Quang Ngai and just across its northern border, in Quang Tin. During my travels in Quang Ngai Province, I learned from civilian officials that since the Marines arrived, in 1965, military operations had swelled the number of people in government "refugee camps" by over a hundred thousand, bringing the official count of these people to a hundred and thirty-eight thousand around the middle of August. The American and Vietnamese officials who managed the camps estimated that about forty per cent of the province's population had passed through the camps during the preceding two years. Over the same period, the Marines, the Army, the Korean Marines, and the ARVN had destroyed approximately seventy per cent of the villages in the province—which means seventy per cent of the houses. I first became aware of this destruction when I spent several days in early August flying, as a reporter, in the back seat of one or another of several two-seat, single-propeller Cessna O-1 Forward Air Control planes (abbreviated FAC, and pronounced "Fac") that flew daily visual-reconnaissance flights over the entire heavily populated coastal strip of the province. (The FAC planes, throughout South Vietnam, were always flown by Air Force pilots.) Some of the planes flew over single districts once a day for several weeks at a stretch, and the pilots became very closely acquainted with the terrain. Whenever it was possible, I checked my estimates of the percentage of houses destroyed against their estimates. In several districts, I was also able to check my estimates with the local ground commanders, although no figures of this kind were kept officially. From the FAC plane's prescribed flying altitude, which was fifteen hundred feet, I found it difficult to distinguish people, unless they were wearing their large brown conical straw hats, but I could easily distinguish houses and the remains of houses. The houses in Quang Ngai had been loosely grouped in groves of trees that stood out like dark-green islands in an expanse of lighter-green or yellow rice fields. From the air, the roofs of houses that were still standing appeared as dark-brown squares; the ashes of houses that had been recently burned appeared as gray squares; and the rain-washed clay foundations of houses that had been destroyed more than a month or so earlier appeared as red or yellow squares. When houses had been burned by troops on the ground, their walls—of clay-and-bamboo or stone—were usually still standing, but the walls of houses that had been bombed or bulldozed were flattened, or strewn over the rice fields. The pattern of destruction was roughly the same throughout the densely populated area of fields and villages lying between the mountains and the sea. Villages remained standing in a long belt a few kilometres wide bordering Route 1, a partly paved two-lane road running the full length of the coastal strip and approximately bisecting it. The rest—with certain exceptions, which I will mention—had been destroyed.

In Binh Son, the northernmost district of Quang Ngai Province, beyond a belt about two kilometres wide along the road, the houses that had stood on the flatland to the west of the road had been destroyed all the way down to the Song Tra Bong ("*song*" is a Vietnamese word for "river"). In the Song Tra Bong Valley, which had formerly been cultivated as far as about fifteen kilometres inland, between the mountains, the houses on the north side of the river had been destroyed as far as about ten kilometres inland. Beyond this, deep in the mountains, the town of Tra Bong, which had a population of several thousand and was also the site of a large Special Forces camp, remained standing. The Special Forces camp stood apart from the village, on a small hill. Bare of trees and grass, the camp was ringed by several rows of barbed wire, outside which were fences of sharpened bamboo poles, with rows of zigzagging trenches outside these. Inside all this was a cluster of low, heavily sandbagged huts with tin roofs. To the east of Route 1, in Binh Son District, beyond the belt of undestroyed houses along the road, seventy or eighty per cent of the houses had been destroyed all the way to the sea. South of the Song Tra Bong, in Son Tinh District, which was the Tactical Area of Responsibility of the Korean Marines, the situation was much the same. Along the south side of the Song Tra Bong, there was a Revolutionary Development project near the village of An Diem, about five kilometres west of the road, and the houses remained standing along this stretch of the river, although, as I have noted, the houses right across it on the north side, in the Tactical Area of Responsibility of the 196th Light Brigade, had been destroyed. On the coastal side of Route 1 in Son Tinh—again excepting the belt of a few kilometres along the road—from eighty to ninety per cent of the houses had been destroyed all the way to the sea. Along the Song Tra Khuc, which marks the southern border of Son Tinh District, the houses remained standing as far as ten kilometres away from the road on the mountain side, but beyond that, starting at the point where the river valley begins to wind between the mountains, they had been destroyed. Within one wide bend of the river, which described a full horseshoe, I could see networks of trenches that had been built by the National Liberation Front running down the center of many villages, and sometimes linking two or more of them. Throughout the province, I saw the black entrances to caves and networks of tunnels, which the entire population used as bomb shelters, and which the N.L.F. used as bunkers, hiding places, and escape routes, but in this bend of the river they were particularly numerous. Still deeper in the mountains, the village of Phuoc Tho remained standing, next to a Special Forces camp on a hill. All the houses of the village were crowded together in a square a hundred metres on a side, which was surrounded by a trench, and single houses out in the fields had been razed. This indicated that Phuoc Tho had been converted into a strategic hamlet. Like most of the province, the valley of the Song Tra Khuc was spotted with craters of all sizes. Craters from artillery fire, which were a yard or two wide, peppered the rice fields and the former villages, and craters from delayed-fuse bombs, which were as much as thirty feet across and seven feet deep, and many of which had filled with water, dotted the landscape with little ponds. Anti-personnel bombs, which explode on contact, had made shallow craters that spread out in rays across the fields, like giant yellow asterisks, and napalm strikes had blackened the fields in uneven splotches. What had formerly been dense woods on the mountainsides that rose up from the cultivated valley in a series of delicate ridges were just as badly torn up.

The two districts to the south of the Song Tra Khuc—Nghia Hanh and Tu Nghia—which were the ARVN's Tactical Area of Responsibility, were the least heavily destroyed of Quang Ngai's districts. Quang Ngai City formed the center of a large undestroyed pocket that extended eastward all the way to the coast and, in places, extended westward along the south bank of the Song Tra Khuc almost all the way to the mountains. In the southern half of Nghia Hanh District, however, there had been considerable destruction near the mountains. To the south of these two least heavily destroyed of the province's districts, and divided from them by the slow-moving Song Ve, are Mo Duc and Duc Pho Districts, which were the Tactical Area of Responsibility of the 3rd Brigade of the 4th Division and were the most heavily destroyed of the province's districts. Except in four small areas, from ninety to a hundred per cent of the houses in these two districts had been destroyed, along Route 1 as well as away from it. The less heavily destroyed areas consisted of an intact stretch about four kilometres in diameter around the village of Mo Duc; a strip about seven kilometres wide extending north from the town of Duc Pho along the western side of Route 1 for about five kilometres, where about half the houses remained standing; the southernmost fifteen kilometres of the coastline, where, again, about half the houses remained standing; and, finally, a region three or four kilometres long and wide around the Song Tra Kau—a small river just north of Duc Pho—and near the mountains, where about sixty per cent of the houses remained standing. As I flew over the coast of Mo Duc District, where over ninety per cent of the houses had been destroyed, I asked the pilot about the people who had lived there, and he answered, "All the personnel that were down there were pretty much V.C."

The villages had been destroyed in many ways and in a great variety of circumstances—at first by our Marines and later by our Army. In accordance with the local policy of the 3rd Marine Amphibious Force, a village could be bombed immediately and without the issuing of any warning to the villagers if American or other friendly troops or aircraft had received fire from within it. This fire might consist of a few sniper shots or of a heavy attack by the enemy. Whatever the provocation from the village, the volume of firepower brought to bear in response was so great that in almost every case the village was completely destroyed. A village could also be destroyed if intelligence reports indicated that the villagers had been supporting the Vietcong by offering them food and labor, but in such a case the official 3rd Marine Amphibious Force rules of engagement required that our Psychological Warfare Office send a plane to warn the villagers, either by dropping leaflets or by making an airborne announcement. Because it was impossible to print rapidly enough a leaflet addressed to a specific village and specifying a precise time for bombing, the Psychological Warfare people had largely abandoned leaflet drops as a method of warning, and had begun to rely almost completely on airborne announcements. There was no official ruling on when troops on the ground were permitted to burn a village, but, generally speaking, this occurred most often after fire had been received from the village, or when the province chief had given a specific order in advance for its destruction. In some cases, the villagers had been removed from an area in a big-scale operation and then the area had been systematically destroyed. By the beginning of September, there had been two large Army operations of this kind. Five thousand inhabitants of the valley of the Song Ve were made to leave their homes. In Binh Son District, along ten kilometres of coastline south of the former village of Tuyet Diem, five thousand people were "extracted." But for the most part the destruction occurred sporadically and piecemeal, without a guiding plan. Although most of the villages in the province had been destroyed, the destruction of villages in large areas was not ordinarily an objective of the military operations but was viewed as, in the words of one official, "a side effect" of hunting the enemy.

When I attempted to find a record of what the Marines had done in Quang Ngai during their two years of operation before Task Force Oregon arrived, I met with very little success. The Information Officers of the units in Task Force Oregon were unable to name any operations that had been conducted by the Marines, and they did not possess any record of casualties, enemy or friendly. Several times, in August, while I was flying over areas where the remnants of fields, forests, and villages were densely pockmarked with half-overgrown craters from the days of Marine operations, I asked the Forward Air Control pilots what operations had been launched in the areas, but they were unable to tell me when, or why, the areas had been bombed.

I met one man who had worked as a Psychological Warfare Officer with the Marines when they first arrived in Duc Pho. He said that for the first month they had been unable to travel five hundred yards beyond their camp without running into heavy enemy fire. After receiving reinforcements, they had moved out farther but had still been unable to penetrate many areas. When the Marines had developed a system in which they took reprisals against the rural people by bombing villages that were thought to be giving support to the National Liberation Front, Leaflet No. 244-286-67 announced this system to the villagers. Its title is listed in a catalogue of Psychological Warfare leaflets used by the Marines and by Task Force

Oregon in Quang Ngai as "Marine Ultimatum to Vietnamese People," and its target is listed as "Civilian Population." The text of the leaflet, like that of all such leaflets, is printed, of course, in Vietnamese. On one side there are two cartoon drawings. The first shows several soldiers of the Vietcong setting up a mortar position near a thatch-roofed house while another soldier leans out of a window firing an automatic weapon. A woman holding a child by the hand stands next to the house. Under the picture, a caption reads, "If the Vietcong do this . . ." The second picture shows an Air Force jet pulling out of its dive over the house. An explosion in front of the house has thrown the soldiers and the woman and her child to the ground, and the house is aflame. In the foreground, a man lies on the earth, clutching his chest. Streams of blood flow from his eyes, nostrils, mouth, and ears. The rest of the pamphlet is in black and white, but this blood is printed in red ink. The second caption, completing the unfinished sentence of the first, reads, ". . . your village will look like this." On the other side is a text reading:

DEAR CITIZENS:

The U.S. Marines are fighting alongside the Government of Vietnam forces in Duc Pho in order to give the Vietnamese people a chance to live a free, happy life, without fear of hunger and suffering. But many Vietnamese have paid with their lives and their homes have been destroyed because they helped the Vietcong in an attempt to enslave the Vietnamese people. Many hamlets have been destroyed because these villages harbored the Vietcong.

The hamlets of Hai Mon, Hai Tan, Sa Binh, Tan Binh, and many others have been destroyed because of this. We will not hesitate to destroy every hamlet that helps the Vietcong, who are powerless to stop the combined might the G.V.N. and its allies.

The U.S. Marines issue this warning: THE U.S. MARINES WILL NOT HESITATE TO DESTROY IMMEDIATELY, ANY VILLAGE OR HAMLET HARBORING THE VIETCONG. WE WILL NOT HESITATE TO DESTROY, IMMEDIATELY, ANY VILLAGE OR HAMLET USED AS A VIETCONG STRONGHOLD TO FIRE AT OUR TROOPS OR AIRCRAFT.

The choice is yours. If you refuse to let the Vietcong use your villages and hamlets as their battlefield, your homes and your lives will be saved.

Peaceful citizens, stay in your homes. Deny your support to the V.C.s.

After a reprisal bombing had been carried out against a village, the Marines sometimes showered it with Leaflet No. 244-068-68. Its title is listed as "Your Village Has Been Bombed," and its target, again, as "Civilian Population." The second picture on the leaflet entitled "Marine Ultimatum to Vietnamese People," which shows the house aflame and the people dead, occupies one whole side of this leaflet. The caption reads, "THE VIETCONG CAUSED THIS TO HAPPEN!" On the other side, the text reads:

ATTENTION VILLAGERS:

1.—Your village was bombed because you harbored Vietcong in your village.

2.—Your village was bombed because you gave help to the Vietcong in your area.

3.—Your village was bombed because you gave food to the Vietcong.

4.—We warned you about the bombings because we did not want to hurt innocent villagers.

5.—Your homes are damaged or destroyed because of the Vietcong.

6.—Your village will be bombed again if you harbor the Vietcong in any way.

7.—You can protect your homes by coöperating with the G.V.N. and the Allied Forces.

8.—Tell the G.V.N. and the Allied Forces where the Vietcong are, so they can protect you.

9.—The G.V.N. and the Allied Forces will drive the Vietcong away from your villages.

10.—The G.V.N. and the Allied Forces will help you to live in peace and to have a happy and prosperous life.

Both the Marines and, after them, Task Force Oregon had originally envisaged a system in which warnings would be issued to the villagers before bombing their village. Most officers I spoke with said that they delivered such warnings whenever they could. The fourth item in the above leaflet and similar passages in many other leaflets concerned with bombings refer to warnings that would allow "innocent villagers" to flee the village. But in practice, of course, when such warnings were delivered, any of the enemy who might be in the village also took the opportunity to leave or to hide underground. And if the enemy had left the village, the bombing became exclusively a reprisal against houses, with no military objective. Rather than carry out a bombing of this kind, which had virtually no chance of killing any enemy soldiers, the American forces often took the course indicated in the "Marine Ultimatum to Vietnamese People," and bombed "immediately," to increase the chance of killing some of the enemy—even if it also increased the chance of killing

19

villagers—and of thereby preserving the partly military character of the target.

Another leaflet, No. 244-055-68, which was ordered by the 1st Marine Regiment, and, like the others, had as its target "Civilian Population," shows a photograph of a field of rubble with a few blackened poles protruding from the earth at odd angles in the foreground. The caption reads, "IF YOU SUPPORT THE VIETCONG . . . YOUR VILLAGE WILL LOOK LIKE THIS." The text on the back reads:

> The U.S. forces have joined with the forces of South Vietnam to rid your villages of Vietcong agents and protect your lives. The Vietcong hide among innocent women and children in your villages to fire upon troops and aircraft. If the Vietcong in this area use you or your village for this purpose, you can expect death from the sky. Do not let your lives and your homes be destroyed. Do not let the Vietcong be the reason for the death of your loved ones.
>
> Report all Vietcong locations immediately. Once the Vietcong are eliminated, peace will come to South Vietnam. Help the G.V.N. help you!

In preparation for some of their ground operations, the Marines dropped Pamphlet No. 44-65, whose title is "Marines Are Friends of Civilians." One side shows a tall Marine shaking hands with a small Vietnamese peasant. The caption is "The U.S. Marines are the friends of the Vietnamese people." The text on the other side reads:

> The Marines are here to help you. Do not run from them! If you run, they may mistake you for a Vietcong and shoot at you. Stand

still and the Marines will not harm you. Tell this to your friends.

At least once, the Marines announced to the press the accidental bombing of what they called a "friendly" village, but they did not mention the intentional bombing of any "unfriendly" villages. The New York *Times* ran the following story on September 28, 1966:

> Two United States Marine Corps planes bombed a friendly village in South Vietnam by mistake yesterday, killing 28 mountain tribesmen and wounding 17, a Marine spokesman said today.
>
> The bombing also destroyed about 100 houses in the village, which is in Quangngai province about 350 miles north of Saigon.
>
> The village was under the control of the South Vietnamese Government, the Marine spokesman said, and was outside the target area for the attack mission to which the two Marine planes had been assigned.
>
> Marine evacuation helicopters went to the village and evacuated the wounded to a Government hospital in the nearby city of Quang-ngai.
>
> The victims were montagnards—the nomadic hill people who furnish large numbers of fighters to help the allied cause.
>
> The Marine spokesman said the village also contained some Government soldiers and their families. . . .

An air strike is not over after a single large explosion that covers the whole target; rather, it involves eight or nine low passes by several fighter-bombers and usually takes from ten to fifteen minutes to complete. Because the

21

pilots of the small propeller Forward Air Control planes observe every pass and help the fighter-bomber pilots adjust for inaccuracies, it is virtually impossible for the full ordnance of an air strike to land on a village simply through poor aim. It may be stated that the accidental bombings that are reported in our press have occurred either because a strike intended for an "unfriendly" village was mistakenly delivered on a "friendly" village or because the Army misjudged the "friendliness" of the village actually bombed. In the case of the bombing reported in the *Times,* the presence of the ARVN soldiers gave incontrovertible proof that the bombed village had been in the "friendly" category.

Task Force Oregon continued the Marines' practice of dropping leaflets threatening to destroy villages that supported the Vietcong. Leaflet No. 244-279-67 uses the two-frame cartoon of a house being bombed, with the caption "If the Vietcong do this . . . your village will look like this," that appears on the "Marine Ultimatum to Vietnamese People." The text on the back reads:

> The military forces of the G.V.N. and the free world have no desire to harm the innocent people of Vietnam who are willing to live in peace. However, if the criminal Vietcong are allowed to hide in your house, both they and your house will be destroyed.

Another leaflet shows a soldier of the Vietcong on his knees, in the foreground, being shot at simultaneously by six jets, two helicopters, two artillery pieces, a tank, and four infantrymen. The caption is "WE MUST DESTROY THE VIETCONG TO HAVE PEACE." The back reads:

> The U.S. forces have come to help the G.V.N. rid your village of the Vietcong who

enslave you. If you allow the V.C. to hide in
your hamlet, you can expect destruction from
the air from mortars and artillery. Do not let
your hamlet be destroyed. Point out the V.C.
who bring death and destruction to you and
your home.

, Other leaflets that were available to Task Force Oregon
for adaptation to its area publicize and condemn damage
caused by the Vietcong. Leaflet No. 244-492-67, whose title
is "Message to the V.C. from the Citizens of Phong Dien
District," shows a photograph of a building with half its
roof blown off. The caption reads, "The Buddhist school
at the Phong Dien Refugee Center lies in ruin following a
senseless V.C. attack on the 15th of May, 1967." The text
on the back reads:

> A MESSAGE TO THE V.C.:
> We the citizens of Phong Dien District will
> never be won over to such a cause as yours. A
> cause that advocates the murder of our people
> and your people. We the citizens of Phong
> Dien beg each of you who have been duped
> by the V.C. propaganda to think of the sorrow
> you have created and forsake this alien cause.
> Would it not be better for you to join with
> us in building our great fatherland under the
> peaceful flag of the G.V.N.?
> THE CITIZENS OF
> PHONG DIEN DISTRICT

The citizens of Phong Dien first became aware of this
message when airplanes dropped it by the tens of thousands over their district.

A number of leaflets issued very detailed instructions to
the population just before an operation began. On one

side of Leaflet No. 244-099-68, which is titled "Instructions to the Citizens of Binh Son District," there is a map consisting of a single line, which represents a five-kilometre stretch of road, and four dots, which represent the villages of Tan Hy, Long Ve, Dong Le, and Phuoc Hoa, from left to right along the road. A red line forms a long, narrow rectangle enclosing the area between the villages of Tan Hy and Phuoc Hoa, which are at opposite ends of the map. The instructions on the back read:

> ATTENTION CITIZENS OF BINH SON DISTRICT:
> The area framed in red on this map is a danger zone. No one may be in this area except on the road. You may not leave the road inside this area. Enter and leave this road outside of the danger zone. Anyone caught within 300 metres of the road between Tan Hy and Phuoc Hoa may be fired upon.
> You must follow the instructions of the G.V.N. The G.V.N. cares about the welfare of the people. The G.V.N. does not want you and your loved ones to be hurt. Obey the laws of your G.V.N.

One almost decisive disadvantage of using leaflets such as this one was that, even if the instructions were coherent and clear, only a tiny minority of the peasants were literate enough to read them at all, and virtually none of the peasants could read maps. When the American Psychological Warfare Officers composed leaflets that told the peasants to flee Communism and come to Saigon government camps, or told them, as one leaflet did, to reject "the Chinese Communist master of the Vietcong," or ordered them to make a choice between the National Liberation Front and the Saigon government, or advised them to boil water before drinking it, it was easy for these officers to forget that, although the enemy was tough and experienced and smart, the majority of the peasants—particularly the women, the children, and the aged—were people who had spent their lives almost wholly within tiny farming communities, and who had no knowledge of the Saigon government's system of camps, of the Chinese Communists, or of the rules of modern hygiene that were described in the leaflets. Often, in addition to assuming literacy and a familiarity with world conflicts on the part of the peasants, the leaflets took it for granted that the peasants shared with the authors of the leaflets a broad range of assumptions about such things as the legitimacy and benevolence of the Saigon government and the criminality of the National Liberation Front.

In late August of 1967, I spent several days in Quang Ngai's southernmost districts, Duc Pho and Mo Duc, which were the Tactical Area of Responsibility of the 3rd Brigade of the 4th Division. First, I visited the brigade headquarters at the Duc Pho base to ask the officers and men of the 3rd of the 4th what resistance they had met from the enemy and how effective they judged their operations to have been, and to ask what had become of the two hundred thousand people who had lived in the two districts before the villages had been destroyed. In a briefing, an officer told me that although few American units had suffered heavy casualties in any single battle, they had suffered heavy casualties over a period of months in hundreds of small encounters with the enemy. He said that from the twenty-second of April to the middle of August a force of eight hundred combat troops directly exposed to enemy fire had suffered six hundred and ten casualties, including a hundred and twenty killed in action. Another officer present put in, "A platoon sergeant can pretty much expect to get hit within three or four months." The briefing officer told me that in the same period the 3rd of the 4th had killed eighteen hundred and seventy-five of the enemy, and captured five hundred and sixty-six firearms. For a month or so, the brigade had kept a tally of what it called "military structures destroyed," but then it had apparently lost interest in these figures, for it had let the statistic of "3,128 military structures destroyed" stand for over a month on a chart in the commanding officer's briefing tent, without bringing it up to date. "We just stopped keeping track after the first month," the briefing officer said.

A high-ranking officer expressed deep concern over the situation in Duc Pho and Mo Duc Districts. When I asked him what had happened to the people living in the two districts, he told me, "We estimate that there are a hundred thousand people living in Duc Pho. We have about twenty thousand living in refugee camps and twenty-eight thousand more living in towns along Route 1; these are our safe areas. That means that we have about fifty-two thousand people still living in zones that we send harassment-and-interdiction fire into through the night. And there has been no attempt to provide security for any of the villages there. We pull out of a village a few hours or days after we go in. Except for the towns of Mo Duc and Duc Pho and the strip of coastline that stretches south from here—it's only about one-half destroyed—these districts are pretty well torn up. The question is: Where do we go from here? ARVN troops are supposed to be doing the Pacification—to go into a village after we have gone through it—but they just can't do it. They aren't here. But, I mean, don't get the idea that we are the only people doing this. Have you been down in Binh Duong Province? The 1st Cavalry Division has wiped out every village it got sniper fire from down there. We're so damned stuck on this body count. If only people could get their minds off that for a while and look at the four hundred defectors, which are the really important thing. But I'll tell you one thing: We haven't been winning any hearts and minds out there, that's for sure. And, you know, the ARVN—they don't care what you destroy. General Hoang Xuan Lam, the commander of I Corps, came down to look at these districts, and when he saw how the place was torn up, he just said, 'Good! Good! They are all V.C. Kill them!' " The officer made a dour face and shook his head. "We sometimes call off strikes because women and children are there. As far as I'm concerned, this idea that women and children are V.C. just doesn't go. A few months ago, we moved a lot of people out of their villages in helicopters before we burned the places, but when we got those villagers to Duc Pho the refugee people said they just couldn't handle them, because they already had too many people for the amount of food and tin roofing they had, so they released the people we'd moved in, and those people went back out there to live underground."

I asked the officer whether he thought the 3rd of the 4th had found an effective way of furthering American war goals in South Vietnam.

Instead of answering, the officer returned the question to me. "What would *you* do with this mission, and this size force in this area?" he asked.

A Psychological Warfare Officer who had worked with the 3rd of the 4th related, "You'll think I'm pulling your leg, but sometimes when we'd planned an air strike on a village, the day before, or the week before, or something, the FAC would be flying over there and notice *people* walking around. You see, that was an area where there wasn't *supposed* to be any people. They wasn't *supposed* to be there. So we would go up there on a chopper an hour before the strike and tell the people to *didi* on out of there." *"Didi"* is Vietnamese for "get out," and is a standard word in American pidgin Vietnamese. "And you'd see 'em puttin' their little sticks on their shoulders, and gettin' their buffalo, and *didi*-in' out. It worked. The 3rd of the 4th was real good about that. Sometimes it don't happen that way. A lot of units will just say 'Unpopulated area— screw it!' and put in the air strikes. But, like I say, the 3rd of the 4th was real good—understandin' the people, and all. The rule is that you have to send a Psy War plane over a village before you hit it unless you get fire, and then you can hit it right away, without askin' anybody. Of course, every once in a while the guys on the ground might burn a couple of hootches that they wasn't supposed to, but that happens everywhere." "Hootch" is military slang for a Vietnamese house. "When they been out in the field a while, they get a little short-tempered, if you know what I mean. You can hardly blame them. This is the toughest damn war we ever fought. In most wars, you could just walk through the place and shoot up everything, but here you can't tell. You just don't know who's with you and who's against you."

One night, I visited the 3rd of the 4th's Fire Direction Center, and learned that on the Duc Pho base alone the brigade had three batteries of six howitzers each and one battery of two eight-inch guns and two 175-mm. guns. A major who was on duty that night told me that there were several ways of deciding on targets. Ground troops could call for artillery fire at any time, and these requests were given the highest priority. But by far the most frequent type of fire was that known as harassment-and-interdiction fire, or h.-and-i. fire, which the major described to me as "a kind of intelligence fire." He went on to explain, "It's not really worthwhile blasting the place through the night. So we just put a shot in now and then. Sometimes we'll get a specific target for h.-and-i. fire, but just as often they'll give us a block five or ten kilometres on a side. At one time or another, we've had these blocks just about everywhere in the district, except along Route 1 in places." The major also told me, "We don't have any unobserved fire. We can put a round through the window of your house if we want to. And I want you to know that we clear everything we fire with the province chief."

I asked what the procedure for obtaining clearance was.

"The province chief marks out the areas where we can't fire without his special permission," he answered, speaking the words "province chief" with extreme gravity. Then he guided me over to a map of Duc Pho and Mo Duc Districts and directed my attention to three strips along Route 1, each about three kilometres wide, that were circled in red. Together, they constituted about forty-four square kilometres of a total of approximately five hundred square kilometres of densely populated flatland between the sea and the mountains that was within the range of guns in the two districts. "Here's the thing that's really important—here's the thing that I want you to see," the major said. "These are the areas for the protection of the friendly Vietnamese civilians. Unless our troops receive fire, we can't shell these areas without specific permission from the Vietnamese province chief.'"

Black circles on the map showed the outer limits of each battery's range of fire. The circles overlapped to cover the entire populated area. Little green dots, designating targets for harassment-and-interdiction fire, were speckled over the whole map except for the three no-fire zones. There were several large green squares, indicating blocks to be "covered" by harassment-and-interdiction fire over a period of days. There was one red box, about two kilometres wide and four kilometres long, around an area consisting of rice fields along with several villages. The major explained that this was a "free-fire zone." Most officers referred to areas that were hit regularly by harassment-and-interdiction fire as "free-fire zones," but at the artillery center, since almost the entire populated territory in the two districts was being hit by harassment-and-interdiction fire, the men had recently restricted the application of this term to a few isolated areas. In its new, narrower definition, it meant simply a harassment-and-interdiction zone where the target was considered particularly "lucrative," and was therefore to be hit quickly with a particularly heavy volume of fire.

I had observed artillery fire from a FAC plane, and had seen that the first few rounds were usually from two hundred to three hundred metres off target. I asked the major about this.

"Yes," he said. "The first few rounds are about two hundred or three hundred metres off, but then the forward observer tells us how far off we are, and we can adjust it to a pinpoint."

I asked what the margin of safety for ground troops was, in average circumstances.

"A thousand metres," he answered. "In tight situations, we'll put it in as close as four hundred or six hundred metres, but that's real hairy. That's the real danger zone."

A chart on the wall listed eight types of fire and the number of missions that had been fired in the three and a half months since the 3rd of the 4th had arrived in Duc

Pho and Mo Duc Districts. (A mission averaged nine shells.) From top to bottom, the chart read:

TYPE OF FIRE	NUMBER OF MISSIONS
Registration	266
H & I	6266
Destruction	7
Prep	30
TOT	109
WA	66
Defensive concentration	328
Others	44

I asked the major to explain the differences between the types of fire.

"Registration fire is to check the accuracy of the gun," he replied. "We pick a spot that's easily recognizable both on a map and from the ground or air. Then we set our guns to what *should* be right, and when we see how far off the shells land we adjust the gun's aiming device to correct any inaccuracies. Junctions of streams provide good, clear targets for registration fire. So do road junctions, but we sometimes have trouble getting clearance for those." He laughed. "H.-and-i. fire can originate with just about anyone, and we just make a general clearance check for that. That is, we check to see if there are any friendlies in the area." By "friendlies" he meant United States or Korean or ARVN troops. He continued, "Destruction fire is when someone says 'I want that bunker.' A specific point on the ground. Some kinds of fire are considered on target within about three hundred metres of the coördinate. 'Prep' is preparation fire. It's the fire we put on a landing zone before the troops go in. 'TOT' fire means 'Time on

Target' fire. It's a kind of artillery surprise attack. We set all our batteries on the same target, decide on a time, and then fire them all out at once. 'WA' means 'Will Adjust.' This is fire where they want to make sure where it goes, so they have a forward observer, or someone else, who actually observes where the shells are landing, and tells the battery how far off they are."

I asked the major whether this meant that other types of fire went unobserved.

"When I said that all fire was observed, what I meant was that someone always sees the target sometime before it's hit," the major answered, and he went on, "Defensive concentration fire is put down all around the company when they are bedding down for the night. First, we put in some check rounds to get the fire on target, and then, if there is trouble later at night, the gun is already adjusted and the fire is there."

In the three and a half months since the 3rd of the 4th had arrived, the batteries at Duc Pho alone had fired 64,044 shells into the populated flatlands of Mo Duc and Duc Pho Districts. (This figure does not include shells fired by the Navy from the South China Sea, or shells fired from batteries taken out into the field to supply direct support to operations.) Another chart listed the number of enemy "KIA" (for "Killed in Action") and "WIA" (for "Wounded in Action") credited to each of the batteries. "We just keep this count for ourselves," the major explained. "Actually, we don't get any credit for the kills. The ground troops get all the credit for the kills." He said that the most commonly used shell, the 105-mm., would kill anything within a radius of thirty-five metres on unobstructed flat ground, and the largest shell, the 8-inch, would kill anything within a radius of seventy-five metres under the same conditions.

An article in the August 16th edition of the *Screaming Eagle,* the weekly newspaper of the 1st Brigade of the 101st Airborne Division, gives an indication of the freedom with which artillery has been used in Duc Pho District. The headline is "RED LEGS CELEBRATE ON ENEMY" ("Red Leg" is the radio call sign for "artillery") , and the article reads:

> DUC PHO (2/320-IO) —What began as a ceremony to fire its 250,000th round turned out to be a fire mission for the 2nd Bn., 320th Arty. recently.
>
> On a mountain-top overlooking the Song Ve river valley, B Btry. was poised for the ceremony. Lt. Col. Andrew Bolcar, Knoxville, Tenn., stood near the 105 howitzer, lanyard in hand. Nearby the color guard stood at attention, flags blowing in the breeze. The ceremony was about to begin.
>
> Then a message came up from the fire direction center. B Co. of the 2nd Bn., 327th Inf., had made contact with the enemy and needed artillery support. Commands were given and adjustments made on the gun sightings. Colonel Bolcar pulled the lanyard and the 250,000th round was on its way to enemy positions.
>
> "There couldn't have been a better way to fire a milestone round than at the enemy," said Bolcar.

The *Screaming Eagle* does not say where the two-hundred-and-fifty-thousandth round was headed before the decision was made to fire it at the enemy.

That same night, to make further inquiries about the estimated fifty-two thousand people who still lived in areas that were being shelled with artillery fire in Duc Pho, I visited Captain Converse B. Smith, who was in charge of the 3rd of the 4th's Civil Affairs Office. Captain Smith, a tall, blond, heavy-boned ex-professional boxer, told me that the Marines had "generated ten thousand refugees" in Duc Pho before the 3rd of the 4th arrived, and that operations of the 3rd of the 4th had swelled the number to twenty thousand. "We haven't been able to do any resettling yet," he said. "The district doesn't have enough troops. We can't secure areas yet. The trouble is that we weren't included in the plan for Pacification and Revolutionary Development for 1967. When Task Force Oregon came, the money wasn't available at the provincial level. They didn't think that we would be ready for it yet. But these districts are ready now for a tremendous Pacification Program. Those people who are still out there had a choice. If they want to come into the secured area, they can come in."

I asked him about the people who had been brought into the camps and then released again.

"We never turn away anyone who says that he *wants* to stay," he answered. "But what are we going to do? When our boys get into a fight, we can't just let the women and children get killed out there, so we bring them in. They are taken to the police and talk to the refugee people, but some of them are inevitably ticked off, and take their sticks on their shoulders and go on back. A lot of times, villagers will allow the V.C. to fight from their village, but they are released again after they are taken and interrogated, even though we *know* that they are V.C. A couple of times, we took the same people out of the same general area three or four times, but they didn't lock them up. We *know* they are all V.C., but the interrogators let them go back again."

I asked Captain Smith whether he expected the villagers to support our Army.

"It boils down to this—they've got to make a decision, one side or the other," he said. "We're here to support the government of South Vietnam, and they are the citizens, and if they want to end this war and get the V.C. killed *they've got to decide*. They can tell us when the V.C. come into the village. They have to stop giving the V.C. food and letting the V.C. fight from their villages. Many Vietnamese get apathetic. This is a feeling that unfortunately many people have in this country. We've got the same problem back in our country. We're spilling blood over here, but a lot of the people don't seem to care."

I asked Captain Smith how he expected a villager to inform on the Vietcong to our soldiers when we could not protect him in his village afterward.

"We have a secret informing system," the Captain replied. "We have many secret contacts. The V.C. don't know about it. And the people have had a chance to come to the government-controlled areas if they wanted to. It is up to them to tell us."

The commonest tactic of large-scale American military operations in Quang Ngai was to suddenly lift troops in on all sides of a reported enemy unit in an attempt to close a trap on it and destroy it. By the end of August, the 1st Brigade of the 101st Airborne Division had attempted three times in Quang Ngai, and also once in Quang Tin, to trap a large enemy force in this way—first in Operation Malheur I, next in Operation Malheur II, then in Operation Hood River, and, finally, in Operation Benton, this last being in Quang Tin—but in each case the trap had closed empty, and the brigade had had to measure the success of the operation by the amount of small-unit fighting it encountered, which was often considerable. In Duc Pho and Mo Duc Districts, the 3rd Brigade of the 4th Division had been fighting on a different principle. Instead of conducting large sweeps according to a detailed plan, it had been sending many company-size units into different parts of the field simultaneously and maneuvering them according to day-to-day assessments of the situation in each small area. On the briefing maps, the paths of a half-dozen units twisted, turned, and doubled back on each other. By the end of August, all the units were operating in an area where most of the villages had already been destroyed, and a great part of their effort consisted in searching for the enemy in networks of tunnels that honeycombed the area.

This area included the region in which it had been estimated that there were still some fifty-two thousand people living, and because these people used the tunnels as their dwellings, and also hid in them when air strikes, artillery fire, or ground fire alerted them to the approach of American troops, the greatest problem that the 3rd of the 4th faced in conducting tunnel warfare was to distinguish enemy soldiers from civilians. Furthermore, the reprisals against the villages had impelled a number of women, old people, and children to take up arms against our troops. Many Vietnamese of the district threw their lives away in desperate, impossible attacks on our troops—attacks that were apparently motivated by pure rage. I heard one officer tell wonderingly of two old men who had rushed a tank column carrying only rifles. "That's when I stopped worrying about shooting the old men," he added. A G.I. told me that he had discovered an old woman trying—and failing—to fire a machine gun at his unit while two small children attempted to guide the ammunition belt into the firing chamber. In the mountain valleys, there had been several cases of attacks with bows and arrows.

Of the civilians in general, an officer related, "We've had tremendous difficulty in hunting them out of the tunnels. We usually try to persuade them with loudspeaker teams to come out, but they just won't. So sometimes we pump tear gas into the tunnel and then blow the place up. I remember once there were several people in the tunnel and we sent down two V.C. defectors in front of our tunnel rat." "Tunnel rat" is a nickname given to American soldiers—usually small soldiers—who have been chosen to enter the tunnels to search for supplies and for the enemy. "After they had gone down about two levels, someone in there fired on them. They came out and we talked some more with loudspeakers, but whoever was down there wouldn't come out. We must have blown half of that hillside away."

After the teller of the story said this, another officer, who had been listening, leaned over the table and said hurriedly, "Of course, we knew that there were some hard-core V.C. down there with those people."

The first officer continued, "Often the local V.C. will be armed with only one hand grenade. Once, we made an announcement into a tunnel and a grenade flew out and killed one of our soldiers. Then a kid about fourteen years old ran out, and we shot him. The grenade was all he had. But I guess he had completed his mission. He had killed an American."

In the *Screaming Eagle,* which relates each week's most dramatic combat stories, there appeared on August 30th an account of one of the 1st of the 101st's tunnel-warfare episodes during the period when this brigade was conducting Operation Malheur I. Under the headline "CONG YANKS CONG," it read:

> In a day-long hide and seek contest, paratroopers of the 101st Airborne matched Communist resistance with American determination and won the prize—feet first. . . . Spec. 4 Donald R. Kinton, Kreole, Miss., entered the cave and the quartet began enlarging the hole in the cave floor.
>
> Once the hole was expanded, Kinton, armed with a lighted torch, crawled into the tunnel.
>
> He saw a VC about to pull the pin on a grenade. Kinton thrust the burning torch into his face and scrambled out of the tunnel.
>
> The grenade was a dud.
>
> Disgusted with the stubborn enemy, the paratroopers dropped several grenades into the tunnel opening.
>
> When the smoke and dust cleared away, one VC crawled out of the hole and surrendered.
>
> . . .
>
> Legari [Pfc. Vito Legari, West Islip, Long Island, New York] decided to enter the tunnel for a look around. An enemy bullet zipped by his head.
>
> The paratroopers pulled back to map new strategy. Third Platoon joined them in suggesting tactics they hoped would force the stubborn enemy to surrender.
>
> A Claymore [a mine that can be aimed to project steel pellets in a given direction] was set off in the tunnel opening.
>
> The VC responded by throwing out a grenade.

Another dud.

The prisoner was sent back to the tunnel opening where he tried to talk his comrades into surrendering.

Nothing happened.

In contempt, Staff Sgt. James A. Ross, Canton, Ohio, dropped another grenade into the tunnel and brought the prisoner back again to persuade them to surrender.

One of the hesitant VC responded, bringing two weapons with him. He explained there was one Viet Cong left in the tunnel and two dead.

Apparently, the report of one remaining stubborn VC was too much for Mr. Pham Minh Cong, interpreter working with "A" Company.

In anger, Mr. Cong threw his helmet to the ground, went into the tunnel and came back dragging the last VC by his heels.

It had taken nearly all day to capture the three prisoners, but it was worth it. The platoon had captured an area VC commander, his assistant, 70 pounds of documents, more than 700 pounds of rice, a typewriter, and medical supplies.

In conversations and in the *Screaming Eagle* I found very little hatred for the enemy expressed. More often, I heard expressions of respect, especially when the enemy was compared to the Vietnamese we were supporting and working with. Nonetheless, most officers spoke of very high morale among our troops. The August 16th edition of the *Screaming Eagle* ran an article on the high morale of some veteran troops which gives a picture of an attitude that the

101st's leadership regarded as a good one for the troops to have toward their work and the war. The article reads:

> Duc Pho—Three paratroopers of the 101st Airborne have the unusual distinction of serving two continuous years in the same unit under seven different commanders. Each has extended his tour of duty in Vietnam a minimum of two times.
>
> Staff Sgt. James Howard, Detroit, Staff Sgt. Pablo Gonzales, San Antonio, and Spec. 4 Roger W. Drought, Janesville, Wis., have been with Troop A of the 2nd Sqdn. (Abn), 17th Cav. since the 101st arrived in Vietnam in July, 1965.
>
> "We sailed over on the USNS General Leroy Eltige," said Drought. "The trip took 22 days and, as I recall, we ran out of fresh water."
>
> The three men have been everywhere in Vietnam the 101st has been sent. They agree the stay at Tuy Hoa, one of the 25 locations occupied by the Screaming Eagles, was the best.
>
> "Tuy Hoa was great," said Drought. "There was a nice beach, a nice town, and plenty of action in the field."
>
> The constant moving doesn't bother them.
>
> "It's just another day's work," said Gonzales. "I've been doing it now for 20 years."
>
> "You get used to it," added Drought. "You even begin to look forward to the moves."
>
> Each paratrooper has seen seven troop commanders come and go. "They've all been good commanders and we have a great unit," said Gonzales. "But then we're prejudiced, having been in it for two years."

Why do men extend tours in Vietnam? The three paratroopers each had their reasons.

"Work here is better than the spit and polish of stateside duty," said Drought. "Here you can see more results of your work."

Howard believes soldiering in Vietnam to be more realistic. "When you go on alert here," he says, "it's the real thing."

Gonzales, close to retirement, thinks Vietnam is the place for a career soldier to be. "I just felt I should finish my Army career here," he said.

The three paratroopers have seen friends leave and return.

"Right now there are guys back in the brigade who have come back," said Drought. He plans to extend again and, perhaps, again.

"I encourage a man to stay if it can benefit his career," said Howard, whose tour is up in August, but [who] is considering staying. "But then no one has ever really tried to talk me into going home," he smiled.

Most of the American soldiers I met in Vietnam supported the war effort as a whole, but I also met a number who expressed doubts. One evening in late August, at the Duc Pho base, I joined a group of four draftees who had entered a small shack to get out of a heavy rain that had continued all day and was turning the base into a sea of mud. They were engaged in a lively argument about the war. Two were deeply disturbed by the war, one was doubtful about certain aspects of it, and one supported it enthusiastically. The conversation was being carried on principally between the two men who were most deeply disturbed—Brandt and Sproul, I will call them. The man who supported the war—I will call him Dehlinger—only looked up occasionally from a pistol he was cleaning to interject a few remarks. The fourth man, whom I will call Jackson, also had comparatively little to say.

"When I got here, some of the villages were wiped out, but quite a lot were still there," said Brandt, a private from California. "Then every time I went out there were a few less, and now the whole place is wiped out as far as you can see. The G.I.s are supposed to win the people's confidence, but they weren't *taught* any of that stuff. I went through that training, and I learned how to take my weapon apart and put it back together again, and how to shoot, but no one ever told me a thing about having to *love* people who look different from us and who've got an ideological orientation that's about a hundred and eighty degrees different from us. We don't understand what they're thinking. When we got here, we landed on a different planet. In Germany and Japan, I guess there was a thread of contact, but even when a Vietnamese guy speaks perfect English *I* don't know what the hell he's talking about."

"No one has any feelings for the Vietnamese," said Sproul, a private from Texas. "They're lost. The trouble is, no one sees the Vietnamese as people. They're not people. Therefore, it doesn't matter what you do to them."

"We interrogate our prisoners in the field, and if they don't coöperate, that's it," said Brandt. "Our prisoners are usually people that we have just picked up in a hamlet that should've been cleared. But there are insufficient facilities for the people in the refugee camps, so they come back, and they're automatically considered V.C. Then we give it to 'em."

"Those V.C.s are hard to break," said Sproul. "One time, I seen a real vicious sarge tie a V.C. upside down by the feet to the runners of a chopper and drag him three thousand feet in the air, swinging out over the paddies. When he came down, hell, he was blabbering it. Another time, I seen them get a bunch of V.C.s in a chopper. They push out one first, and then tell the others that if they don't talk they go out with him. And they talk."

I asked Sproul what he was going to tell people about the war when he returned to the United States.

"Maybe when I go home I'll just crawl back inside myself, and not say a word," he answered. "Things are so violent nobody would believe it. And I don't want to die of frustration trying to convince them."

(The remark "They wouldn't believe it back home" was one that I heard almost every day in Quang Ngai, from the many who supported the war as well as from the minority who did not. While I was riding in a jeep at the Chu Lai base, the driver, who had spent time in the field, suddenly turned to me and said, "You wouldn't believe the things that go on in this war."

"What things?" I asked.

"You wouldn't believe it," he said, with finality.

"What kind of things, then?" I asked.

"You wouldn't believe it, so I'm not going to tell you," he said, shaking his head to show his determination not to tell me. "No one's ever going to find out about some things, and after this war is over, and we've all gone home, no one is ever going to know."

I could not persuade him to elaborate.)

In response to what Sproul had said, Jackson, who was from Georgia, spoke up. "I know. I've seen all that stuff. I've seen the G.I.s out in the field get angry and beat people up—women and all—but I just turn myself off. I know it's wrong, but I just don't say anything about it."

The conversation in the shack turned to the question of whether we should be in Vietnam at all. Sproul thought we should not be. Brandt was unhappy with the war, but he was afraid that we might have to fight another war somewhere else if we didn't fight this one. Jackson thought we should drop nuclear bombs on North Vietnam, and on China, too, if necessary, rather than continue to fight what he saw as an unwinnable war in South Vietnam.

When Communist China was mentioned, Dehlinger looked up to say, "They killed a Red Chinese at Kontum."

"How do you know he was a Chinese?" Brandt asked.

"They can tell by the way they look."

"Well, how did they know he was a *Red* Chinese?"

"Any old Chinaman comes from China, doesn't he?" Dehlinger answered, and he went on to say, "I've seen about forty dinks get zapped in the field, and I can tell you that I want to get out there and pop some more dinks!" The four soldiers all laughed at this sudden resolute declaration.

A few minutes later, Brandt said, "Yesterday, I was out on a Medevac"—a Medevac is a helicopter that carries the wounded from the field to hospitals—"and three civilians had got shot up real bad. There was a little boy and two women. One of them was really messed up. She had three or four major bandages. But they were just chuckin' her onto the helicopter like cordwood. There was a strap hanging down from the ceiling of the chopper with a buckle on it, and it slapped the woman in the face as they tossed her in. Now, some G.I. could have pushed that buckle aside and *then* put her in, couldn't he? And her blanket blew off, leaving her sort of half naked. Now, you'd think that some G.I. would have put that blanket *on* again. But no. I remember once, when I was on a ski slope, I broke my leg. It was excruciating! I remember when the guy came along to take off my boot he was real careful not to cause me any more pain, and I really remember that.

You really remember kindness when you're really suffering. Like if someone does something nice for you when your mother dies. That's when you really remember it. They drop those millions of leaflets, but they won't put on the blanket."

On August 19th, I flew in a "bubble," or OH-23, helicopter over the northern twenty kilometres of the coast of Duc Pho and Mo Duc Districts, and had a chance to view at first hand the areas I had seen on the Duc Pho artillery maps and had been discussing with the men of the 3rd of the 4th for the last several days. The OH-23 seats two people inside a clear-plastic bubble that affords a view in all directions except through a small steel plate underfoot and through the seat backs. The engine sits, uncovered, directly behind the bubble, and supports the long rotor blades on a metal shaft; behind the engine a thin, sticklike tail supports a small rear rotor. The machine rests on narrow metal runners. Originally, the Army had brought the OH-23 to Vietnam strictly for reconnaissance flights, but the 3rd of the 4th had converted it into a gunship by dangling an automatic weapon by a piece of wire in the open doorway on one side of the bubble. The OH-23 pilots, who were Army men, went out daily over the destroyed, but still inhabited, areas on what they called "squirrel-hunting missions," to find the enemy and either kill them with the dangling machine gun or call for artillery fire. They informed me that in the course of three months their body count had reached fifty-two, which was more than the larger Huey gunships of the 3rd of the 4th could claim for that period. "The Huey has to start its run on a target from much farther away than we do, and has to pull off sooner, and it can't fly low at all," a young pilot told me while I was talking with a group of OH-23 pilots.

I asked whether they considered everybody who remained in the destroyed areas to be one of the enemy.

"They've had a chance to get out," the pilots' commanding officer answered. "But they're not *all* V.C., I guess. Sometimes they just go back to their fields. But anyone of military age is a pretty sure bet as a V.C. It's definitely a V.C.-controlled area. We've got shot at in that area ever since we got here. A lot of times, you see a guy taking a shot at you and a woman and kid are standing right nearby. I used to hesitate to call artillery strikes on them, but I'm getting over that now."

The purpose of the flight I went on was only to convey me from the Duc Pho base to the city of Quang Ngai, but the pilot offered to take me on a detour over the areas where he and his fellow-pilots hunted the enemy. Since there was go gunner aboard, it would not be possible to fire on anyone the pilot might identify as a Vietcong soldier during our flight. We left shortly after five o'clock—about half an hour before sunset. Flying in the bubble gives one an entirely different sensation from flying in any other aircraft. In contrast to the Huey helicopter, a ten-passenger craft that takes off and lands slowly and hesitantly, like a boat leaving or approaching a pier, the bubble seems to leap effortlessly into the air, like an elevator in a modern office building. Aloft, you find that as you face forward or to either side no part of the helicopter is visible except the control panel at the front, the tiny floor, and the edge of your seat, which sticks out several inches beyond the edge of the floor. Most helicopters fly over the landscape, above the treetops and house roofs, but the bubble flies *within* the landscape—often among the trees and level with the houses, when they are not too close together. Above rice fields, it easily skims along at an altitude of six or eight feet. Flying in this tiny, agile craft, with all the machinery out of sight behind you, you feel a tremendous freedom to go wherever you please—as though you could alight on a tree branch, like a bird, or fly right in at the door of someone's house and then out through a window.

As we flew east toward the coast, I saw that the destroyed area began on the outskirts of the base. Tracks made by tanks, bulldozers, and armored personnel-carriers criss-crossed the red-earth foundations of the houses; not even the ruins were left standing. We soon passed beyond these former villages and arrived over a wide belt of rice fields lying between Route 1 and the coast. The fields were covered with craters but were still cultivated; people wearing the loose black garment of the Vietnamese peasant were bent over at work in the rows of rice. The fields were littered with scraps of paper, which covered the field divides and had sunk into the shallow water between them. The pilot explained that these were Psychological Warfare leaflets. (An average of a million leaflets were being dropped on Quang Ngai Province every day.) We crossed a tree line at the eastern edge of the rice fields and entered an area where the homes of between twenty and thirty thousand people had been loosely grouped in villages along a coastal strip that was about twenty kilometres long and four kilometres wide. The houses along this strip had been destroyed almost without exception. In the coastal area of Duc Pho District, approximately two-thirds of the houses had clay-and-bamboo walls with thatched roofs, and the rest had stone walls with red tile roofs. Where soldiers had set fire to a house on the ground, the back-yard garden and fence, the well, the hedge, the stone gateposts, and the surrounding palm glade or bamboo grove remained standing, but the house that had provided a focus for this setting, and had received the shade of the trees, was missing; only a square of ashes and debris remained on the foundation. In places where the villages had been shelled, bombed, or strafed, the destruction had not been so selective. "General-purpose" bombs had sent out hails of steel fragments and shock waves, and, near their craters, the upward force of the blasts had torn off the leafy tops of the palm trees, leaving only the trunks standing, with their shattered tips pointing at the sky. Shrapnel had cut down many trees halfway up their trunks, or lopped off their branches, or, in places, thrown whole trees fifty or a hundred yards into adjacent fields. In places where napalm had been used, the yards and fields were blackened and leafless in large splotches. Many artillery and bomb craters were partly filled with leaflets that had been carried across the fields by winds. It did not appear that the destruction had been carried out systematically. The ruins of most of the villages displayed the marks of many methods of destruction. Knowing that the artillery often simply "covered" large areas several kilometres on a side with harassment-and-interdiction fire over a period of days, I found the senseless-looking pattern of craters— dotting the open fields as well as the tree lines and the villages—more understandable. Tanks and armored personnel-carriers had cut their own roads through the landscape. Apparently, the drivers had chosen to travel through the fields rather than use the existing roads, which were likely to be mined.

The families who had returned from the camps, or had just stayed on in the area, lived underground. The dark mouths of their caves dotted the tree lines of the back yards. As we flew overhead, whole families sitting in the yards of destroyed houses tilted their heads up and froze in position to watch us out of sight. It was nearly six o'clock now, and many families were crouching around fires, cooking their dinners. Pots, bedding, and a few pieces of furniture lay out in the yards. In some places, the spindly frames of tiny huts had appeared. Everywhere there were mounds of hay about three feet high, and I later found out that these were small, wall-less individual sleeping shelters consisting of straw thatching mounted on sticks. Some people had built their straw shelters out in the center of the fields, away from trees and bunkers—perhaps because they knew that our Army, believing all bunkers and caves to have been constructed by the Vietcong as fortifications, treated them as prime military targets. Firewood, most of it beams from the destroyed houses, lay about in piles. Children played in the dust, and generally there were far more children, women, and old people in sight than men. Small boys were riding in from the fields on the backs of water buffalo. The pilot noticed artillery shells sending up puffs of whitish smoke in several spots near one edge of these fields, and took care to skirt the area by about a kilometre. The people below continued to work outside their shelters and did not show any sign of noticing the artillery shells that were exploding nearby. The pilot flew the bubble out over the rice fields, and we raced across them at a height of fifteen feet. He pointed out a few scraps of twisted metal and machinery lying in a scorched circle in one of the fields and said that his helicopter had been shot down there a month before. He and his gunner had landed without injury. Once they were on the ground, guerrillas had shot at them from a tree line, and they had fired back. Fifteen minutes later, they had been rescued by another helicopter. A minute or so after he'd pointed out the spot where he crashed, he performed one of the bubble's many aerial stunts. He raced toward the tree line and then, when it seemed that we would crash into the trees, suddenly brought the helicopter sharply upward and arrested its forward motion, so that it rolled up over the trees and house ruins and came to a stop in the air as though it had been caught head on by a blast of wind. As we floated slowly just above the half-destroyed trees, the pilot exclaimed, "Look! There's one!" In a rising tone of tense excitement, he continued, "See? See? He's hiding!" I looked down and saw a youth crouching on a path next to a line of trees. The pilot wheeled the bubble and headed it back toward the youth, who then stood up and began to chop at a log with an axe. "See? Now he's pretending to be working!" the pilot said. An instant later, he cried out, "Look! There's another. She's hiding! See how she's hiding?" I looked down and saw that as our bubble drifted in a slow arc a woman in black edged carefully around a thin tree, always keeping on the opposite side of the trunk from the bubble.

We flew inland to the other side of Route 1, where the villages had also been destroyed. Rushing low across the darkening landscape, we passed over a field of tall grass, and the pilot said, "I killed four there. They ran for a bunker, but they didn't make it." We came to a destroyed village that had stood in the shade of rows of trees. A line of smoke rose from an orange dot of flame in a thicket, and the pilot said, "There's a V.C. havin' his supper. There shouldn't be anyone down there. He shouldn't be there." We began to fly a meandering seaward course down the Song Ve, which marked the boundary between the 3rd of the 4th's Area of Responsibility and the South Vietnamese Army's Tactical Area of Responsibility. A naked boy stood washing a smaller naked boy in a broad bend of the river, which was clear, with a sandy bottom. The two froze and watched as our helicopter passed over them. The spans of two bridges lay twisted in the river. On the south bank, where the 3rd of the 4th had been operating, piles of bricks and ashes and skeletons of blackened poles stood on the foundations of houses, and the fields were brown or black, or had gone wild, but on the north bank, where the South Vietnamese Army had been operating, the trees and fields were full and green—it might have been a different season there—and the houses remained standing, next to their vegetable gardens, yards, and palm trees. As we returned toward Route 1, we crossed over to the north bank. Smoke from supper fires rose from dark courtyards. People carrying loads on shoulder poles walked homeward down the sides of the road, and girls glided down other roads on bicycles. When the pilot set me down on a small helicopter pad within the American Advisory compound on the edge of Quang Ngai City, night had fallen. Inside the compound, all was American, and there was nothing to indicate that I had not magically been set down within the United States itself.

The buildings of the compound were of white clapboard, and neatly ordered, and the busy sound of conversation floated out of a brightly lit dining hall, where food was being served buffet style. Soldiers and civilian advisers with fresh shirts and neatly combed hair laughed and chatted as they entered an air-conditioned movie theatre. I went into the officers' bar and sat down next to a table of officers who were singing as they drank. Their voices were loud and unrestrained, and they banged their glasses on the table to keep time. The lyrics of one of the songs—a song that was apparently meant, in part, to ridicule the

51

idea that civilians are unnecessarily killed by our air strikes, and one that I was to hear again, in many variations, during my stay in Quang Ngai—went:

> Bomb the schools and churches.
> Bomb the rice fields, too.
> Show the children in the courtyards
> What napalm can do.

In June, while the 3rd Brigade of the 4th Infantry Division was operating in Duc Pho District, the men of the 1st Brigade of the 101st Airborne Division, whose motto is "No slack," moved to the northwest to launch Operation Malheur II. (The 1st of the 101st named this operation and its predecessor Malheur after a town in Oregon, and not because the word means, in French, "misfortune," or "woe.") Operation Malheur II was the first of a series of three operations in which the 101st moved progressively northward through the three large river valleys that open out into the coastal lowlands of Quang Ngai. (Operation Malheur I had been in Duc Pho.) By killing enemy units in this area, and turning it into a harassment-and-interdiction-fire zone, the 101st hoped to impede the flow of supplies and men between the guerrillas in the lowlands and the guerrillas in the mountains. Malheur II was launched in the valley of the Song Ve, which winds between the mountains for ten or fifteen kilometres. The first step was to move some five thousand people living in the valley to sites nearer the coast, where camps were to be built. The villagers were transported by helicopter, and they were permitted to bring whatever possessions they could carry in their arms.

As in all operations in which American troops evacuated large numbers of civilians from an area of operation, the 101st was faced, in Malheur II, with the task of rapidly categorizing each person according to his estimated degree of involvement in the National Liberation Front. The categories, from the most suspect to the least suspect, were "confirmed V.C.," "V.C. suspect," "V.C. supporter," "detainee," "refugee," and "defector." But in conditions like those prevailing in Malheur II—with the Army Intelligence people working with no more than a half-dozen interpreters and having only a few days to sort out more than five thousand people in an area where the South Vietnamese government had maintained no presence for over a decade and had no knowledge of the people, and where women, children, and old people had been known to take up arms with the N.L.F.—it was virtually impossible, in most cases, for the Army to determine a person's involvement in the N.L.F. It is fair to say that in most cases the Army decided what category a person was to be put in on the basis of what the Army was doing to him at that moment or had just done to him. When the troops entered a village and rounded up the villagers for evacuation, they categorized the villagers as "V.C. supporters" or "V.C. suspects," and categorized the village as "100 per cent V.C.," but when the same villagers were removed to a camp the Army categorized them as "refugees." By the same token, a Vietnamese who had been shot by our troops was almost invariably categorized as a "confirmed V.C." (The soldiers had a joke that ran, "Anything that's dead and isn't white is a V.C.") The practice that had grown up of judging the guilt of a Vietnamese by what we happened to do to him could be clearly seen in the Army's use of the category "detainees." A "detainee" was theoretically a person whose degree of participation in the N.L.F. was unknown and who had been detained simply for interrogation. But in Malheur II the 101st listed the number of "detainees" (there were six hundred and thirty-one) along with the number of enemy killed and prisoners of war taken, as though by detaining them the Army had proved them to be members of the N.L.F. Matters were further confused by a wide overlapping of terms, and extreme ambiguity in their usage. The terms "detainee," "V.C. suspect," and "refugee" could all refer to the same person, depending on how the local commander chose to see him, although the terms were kept separate on statistical charts that were sent to Saigon. In Malheur II, all the "refugees" could certainly be said to have been "detained," and while they were in their villages their area was considered hostile and they were considered to be "V.C. supporters." In the field, the terms "V.C. suspect" and "V.C. supporter" were often used interchangeably. When a man was deemed to be a particularly suspicious "V.C. suspect," the usual procedure was to tie his hands behind his back, tie a sandbag over his head, and send him to an interrogation center. Finding him in this prisonerlike condition, the next people who dealt with him tended to treat him as a confirmed supporter of the enemy, and he was lucky if he escaped torture and imprisonment.

While Malheur II was going on, the 101st organized a project that appealed greatly to the men's sense of humor— a cattle drive. They rounded up more than a thousand head of cattle and water buffalo and began to drive them down the valley toward the camps to which the people had been moved. The project took much longer than had been expected, however; after six days the cattle had travelled only sixteen of the twenty kilometres to the camps. Sick of cattle driving, the 101st turned the herd over to a unit of South Vietnamese local-defense soldiers, or Popular Forces, who stole about two hundred of them and drove the remainder to the stockades near the camps. Some days later, the theft was discovered, whereupon American troops returned and shot many of the stolen cattle.

A brigade press release recounted the evacuation and cattle-drive phases of the operation as follows:

> More than 5,000 residents of the Song Ve River Valley west of here regained their identity with the Republic of Vietnam government as Vietnamese and American military units concluded the largest civil affairs operation ever launched in Quang Ngai Province. . . .
>
> As the villages were evacuated, the joint military force collected cattle and livestock, initiating the second phase of the operation by driving the herd to Nghia Hanh. While helicopters whisked the villagers to Nghia Hanh, paratroopers began the cattle-drive. They dubbed the overland route "The Chisholm Trail," and cries of "head 'em up; move 'em out" echoed through the valley. The Vietnamese forces sang folk songs; the paratroopers replied with western tunes. Private First Class Gary M. Nichols, Wynne, Ark., a dozen hours away from a degree in veterinary medicine, administered to the herd and calves born during the trip.

For release to the press, the brigade selected a photograph that showed soldiers herding the cattle through large paddy fields where young, recently transplanted rice shoots were showing only a few inches above the water, and supplied it with a caption that read, "Rice paddies, not plains." In conversation, officers of the 101st often displayed warm amusement and delight at the idea of transplanting such a typically American thing as a cattle drive into a Vietnamese setting of rice fields.

Several weeks after the completion of Operation Malheur II, I flew over the Song Ve Valley in a FAC plane, and observed that all the houses there had been destroyed. The pilot told me that troops of the 101st had destroyed them after the people had been evacuated. He also pointed out that the fields had turned uniformly brown, and explained that Operation Ranch Hand—the organization that carries out defoliation—had sprayed the valley.

A few days later, I asked the Information Officer of the brigade how the destruction had taken place.

"I'm afraid you've got your information wrong there," he answered. "We didn't destroy that valley."

I told him that I had just flown over the area and had observed that it had been destroyed.

"I don't know about that, but we didn't destroy the valley," he said.

I asked how he accounted for its destruction.

"Well, when we left the valley, it was standing," he said. Then, after a long pause, he added, "We had no *plan* of destroying the valley. But then Charlie went back in there, and we had no choice about it, so we inserted two battalions back into the valley, and then it got destroyed in the process of denying it to the enemy."

The Information Officer at the Task Force Oregon headquarters expressed complete astonishment when he heard that the villages in the valley had been destroyed. "That's a new one on me," he said.

I often found that American officers tended to ignore some of the results of their operations—such as the destruction of the villages in a large area—or even to deny them, if these results hadn't been envisaged in the original optimistic plans they had made for the districts they were operating in.

When the villagers from the Song Ve Valley were landed at the empty lots in Nghia Hanh, where shelter was theoretically to be provided soon, they became part of what was at that time an officially registered population of a hundred and twenty thousand dispossessed people in Quang Ngai Province—people whose minimum needs of shelter and food had not yet begun to be met. In late June, Mr. Ernest Hobson, who held the civilian post of provincial adviser for refugees in Quang Ngai, under U.S. AID, had written in the monthly *Statistical Annex to the Special Joint Report for the Province of Quang Ngai:*

> The most significant problem in the area of refugee service this month was brought about by the military operation of Task Force Oregon, in which the Refugee Service was called upon to specifically support a military action. . . . The mounting problems of inadequate staff, both VN and American, Logistics, and funds cannot be met without substantial emergency assistance from both regional and national headquarters. . . . The aforementioned military action has exceeded camp construction for new refugees. 500 additional units are needed in Nghia Hanh alone.

At the time the people from the Song Ve Valley arrived, there was a severe shortage of emergency rations, and, because of an administrative mixup, the Army did not release until almost a week later some sixty-two tons of rice it had collected in the valley. After four days without food, a number of people who had been placed in a field directly beside one of the storehouses of captured rice attempted to break into it at night. The Army responded with tear-gas grenades, and two twelve-year-old boys were killed. At the end of August, two thousand families in the camps, some of them from the Song Ve Valley, were still without shelter of any kind. In early August, Deputy Ambassador Robert Komer was alerted to the situation by television and newspaper reports, and he wrote a letter, dated August 15th, to Dr. Nguyen Phuc Que, the Saigon government's Commissioner for Refugees. The letter was copied and distributed to some officials in I Corps. (I Corps is the military designation of the five northernmost coastal provinces of South Vietnam.) It read:

> I am sure you agree that the refugee situation in I Corps is serious.
>
> At least one half of the refugees in South Vietnam are in I Corps. There is an intense concern in the U.S. and particularly in our Congress about the details of the situation in I Corps. There have been several newspaper stories and TV reports during the past week in the U.S. on the I Corps situation. I am afraid that the refugee problem in I Corps is outstraining G.V.N. capability to deal with it. There is a shortage of aluminum roofing and other shelter material accentuated by inadequate airlift capability. There is critical need for emergency rice rations. We are told that

less than 50% of the refugees have received
Temporary Relief Payments; less than 25%,
Resettlement Assistance; and that the special
commissariat on refugees is seriously hampered
by lack of interest on the part of many province officials.

The Ambassador went on to suggest a system in which a
high priority would be given to the transportation of
supplies for dispossessed people in I Corps.

Dr. Que, in turn, placed the responsibility for the crisis
on the United States Army. On October 13th, a U.P.I.
dispatch reported Dr. Que as saying that at some of the
camps in I Corps "the food shortage is so severe starvation
is a threat." The dispatch continued:

Dr. Que complained that he frequently gets
only a day's advance warning when U.S. military operations suddenly create thousands of
refugees.

He said he can make no arrangements for
receiving the refugees—sometimes in groups
of 10,000 at a time—when he is not told be-
forehand.

He said 14 military operations so far this
year have generated about 300,000 refugees.

"Only at the last moment—maybe a day or
two before—do I receive a phone call: 'Dr.
Que, there will be 10,000 refugees for you tomorrow at such and such a place.' "

From the "Refugee Relief Operational Handbook,"
which lays down the countrywide rules for dealing with
the dispossessed in South Vietnam, I learned that the term
"temporary relief payment" referred to food and money
that were supposed to be given as an emergency provision
to people who had arrived at the camps. The handbook

states, "The official rate of temporary relief payment, regardless of age and ethnic origin, is VN $10 [about eight cents] per refugee a day. Temporary relief allowances may be paid either wholly in cash or partly in cash and partly in rice." In short, Deputy Ambassador Komer's statement meant that, as of August 15th, over half the people in government camps in I Corps, who numbered more than a half million, had received no food from our government, or the Saigon government, since their arrival in the camps. After the letter had been sent, some emergency assistance was given to I Corps. But between June, when Mr. Hobson wrote his emergency plea, and the end of August the number of people dispossessed by military operations had increased by 31,888 in Quang Ngai alone, and the crisis had become more acute. To help relieve the food shortage in the camps in Duc Pho District, the 3rd Brigade of the 4th Division collected as much as half a ton of leftovers from its mess halls several times each week and distributed this food at nearby camps.

In speaking of the people in the camps, American officials usually avoided any direct reference to the manner in which these civilians were dispossessed, and referred only to "refugees generated," or "refugees from Communism," or "people freed from V.C. domination." The slogan "Two million refugees have voted with their feet for the G.V.N." has become one of the clichés of the war, and the American Office of Civil Operations includes many of these camps in its reports on the number of "secure hamlets." In his August report, Mr. Hobson stated the problem in different terms:

> From June 13, 1967 to date, we have received a total of 31,888 new refugees as a direct result of allied military operations.

Most of these new refugees were in fact evacuees. The meteoric rise in the number of refugees severely taxed the G.V.N.'s capabilities to deal with the situation. There exist serious shortages in rice, U.S. commodities, and roofing material. Region and Saigon find themselves hard-pressed to overcome the critical shortage in roofing material before the onset of the rainy season. Presently there are approximately 2,000 families without adequate housing of any kind.

The June sheet of a mimeographed report called *General Refugee Situation in Province,* which is put out by the South Vietnamese provincial government, classified some 80,000 of 122,680 "refugees" as "scattered," which meant that they had not received shelter within the camps. This sheet stated that there were 122,680 people in or around the camps and that they had been supplied with 573 latrines, 33 schools, and 27 medical dispensaries, or 1 latrine for every 214 people, 1 school for every 3,000 children (calculating the number of children as roughly two-thirds of the "refugees"), and 1 medical dispensary for every 4,543 people. These facilities were not evenly distributed among the camps. Out of 68 camps, 50 had no schools, 46 had no latrines, and 42 had no medical dispensary. Of the 573 latrines, 471 were in camps in Son Tinh District, with the remaining 102 distributed over all the other districts.

An estimated fifteen per cent of the people in the sixty-eight camps were able-bodied men. There were a few jobs available to the women of the camps, mostly on American bases. A number of women became waitresses in the American mess halls, and a number were employed to fill and carry sandbags for the construction of fortifications. All these women were paid a salary. At both the Duc Pho base and the Chu Lai base, prisoners of war also filled sandbags, and were made to labor on fortifications. On the bases, it was a very common thing to see a gang of Vietnamese women out in the sand dunes, filling and carrying sandbags in the hot sun, while an American soldier sat near them holding an M-16; once, on the Chu Lai base, a mine was discovered built into a wall of sandbags that a gang of these dispossessed Vietnamese women had constructed near an ammunition depot. A number of the young women of the camps became part of the population of prostitutes who catered to the Americans. (A town that was right in front of the gates of the Chu Lai base was considered so insecure that the servicemen visited its bars and its prostitutes only between eight and eleven o'clock in the morning.) The few able-bodied men in the camps could find occasional work breaking rocks on the bases. All jobs on the bases were filled according to a daily-pickup system, and workers were hired or laid off as the Army's construction needs changed. Another small group of people from the camps made baskets or curios for the G.I.s to buy as souvenirs. However, all these kinds of work occupied, at most, only a few hundred of the people. The rest remained idle.

Shelter in the camps consisted, typically, of long parallel rows of barrack-shaped, unwalled, floorless frames made of poles and roofed with tin. The people listed as "scattered" slept under low roofs of thatching propped up on poles, or out in the open. Some people built shacks of cardboard boxes, on which the same markings would be repeated again and again. (The walls of several houses read "COMBAT MEAL COMBAT MEAL COMBAT MEAL" from top to bottom.) Because food was a greater necessity than shelter, some of the camp dwellers sold their allotment of tin roofing to people in Quang Ngai City in order to get money for rice, whose price had risen enormously as a result of the sudden increased demand from the camps and the concomitant drop in local production following the abandonment of the land. Provincial and district officials also stole a considerable quantity of tin and sold it in the towns. The main streets of Quang Ngai City glittered with illegal new tin roofs. It was these new tin roofs that alerted American refugee advisers to the fact that much of the tin was not being used in the construction of shelters for the people in the camps. The best-developed camps were some that, in coöperation with American and Vietnamese authorities, were run, and also financially assisted, by the Cao Dai sect of Buddhists. As in the other camps, the shelters were laid out in straight, barracklike rows with treeless aisles running between, but here they usually consisted of clay walls on bamboo frames, and no one slept uncovered. The people in these camps, unlike the rest, had been supplied with a small amount of government land to farm.

The "Refugee Relief Operational Handbook" outlines standard procedures that officials in the Refugee Division of the Office of Civil Operations in Saigon had devised for dealing with the people in the camps. In the handbook's plan, two stages are outlined—Temporary Camps, and Resettlement. Section I-B of Chapter 3 of the handbook lists a number of facilities as "mandatory" for every hundred families in the temporary camps—twenty latrines, one classroom, and two wells, for example. Section I-C of the same chapter lists several temporary-camp activities, including "collective activities, civic action, and civil operations, solidarization of refugees, orientation in democracy," and "vocational training," but in Chapter 4, entitled "Resettlement," the report notes, "Under no circumstances will the construction of vocational training centers be permissible. Arrangements should be made to use government or private housing . . . to avoid unnecessary budget drain." Section II, which is headed "Refugee Registration Procedure," requires that a specialist take fingerprints and photographs of all "unidentified persons." Section IV of Chapter 3 specifies that the temporary relief payment of ten piastres a day may be given for one month, and that an extension of one month may be made "in case local insecurity still prevails, or the construction of re-settlement centers has not been achieved in time." Section IV-B lists people in the following categories as eligible for temporary relief payments:

> 1. Refugees from insecure areas and re-grouped in temporary camps.
> 2. Non-native applicants for temporary shelter [who] should be interrogated for background data and home province-leaving reason. Details of previous relief status should be obtained via a cable from the province of origin for assessment and action. Meanwhile, they are granted provisional shelter at a refugee camp and commodity support only.
> 3. Dependents of cadres . . . and Popular Forces elements . . . coming from insecure areas. . . .
> 4. Dependents of V.C. elements, for humanitarianism's sake; however, the local authorities should keep track of their whereabouts for possible subversive activities.

Although payments to people in the temporary camps are supposed to last only two months, at the longest, the handbook notes that in what are termed "old temporary camps" additional wells and latrines may be needed.

In the second stage outlined in the handbook—"Re-

settlement"—the people in the temporary camps are envisaged as returning to a normal existence in new villages,
with jobs, proper houses, and an effective system of security to protect them from Vietcong influence. Several
methods of resettlement are listed. Of "Return to Village,"
the first method mentioned, the handbook states, "This is
the best resettlement formula. However, the home village
should be completely pacified and absolutely secure to
eliminate the chance of a second exodus." If the displaced
people are from another province, the "host province"
may give them temporary relief payments only if it has
received confirmation from the original province of "the
honesty of their escape from Communism." A second
method of resettlement is titled "Resettlement in Temporary Camps." The handbook says, "If there are no
locations favorable to resettlement in a given province or
Autonomous City, refugees will be resettled at their temporary camp. In this matter, the temporary housing unit
they have occupied to date now becomes their own and
the local administration is excused from paying them VN
$5,000 resettlement housing allowance." Chapter 4, Section
II, Paragraph 2 specifies that resettlement sites "should
have easy access by surface and a vast potential which will
endure a flourishing economy."

At several points, the handbook makes it clear that
people who have been victimized by the Vietcong are to be
treated more generously than people who have been victimized by American military operations or natural disasters. In Chapter 5, which concerns "disaster relief assistance," the handbook specifies that if a person over
eighteen is killed "By V.C.s" his family is to receive four
thousand piastres, but if he meets his death in any other
way—and the handbook lumps all other ways together
under the heading "Caused by Carelessness"—his family is

to receive only three thousand piastres. At the end of this chapter, the handbook states, "The above assistance is only applicable to refugees who have been receiving temporary relief or been permanently resettled for a period of less than one year. In excess of this time limit they are considered as having recovered a normal life."

Late in August, I spoke with Mr. Hobson, a stocky Negro administrator who holds an M.A. in business administration and who before coming to Vietnam as the provincial adviser for refugees had spent several years as a parole officer in the United States and had worked on youth projects in Harlem. "We have completely dropped the ball on these refugees," he told me. "These people have been neglected or abused since they arrived. Right now, I have five thousand people with no roof over their heads. We just don't have the manpower and supply. Of course, these are the worst camps. Our two best camps are supported by the Buddhist sects. Most camps have situations where ten families live in the space for one. And the people have no jobs. Eighty-five per cent of the refugees are women, children, and old people. If they get any land to farm, it's usually the worst land, because government land is always the worst. We've been trying to get a job-training program going, but the basic problem is that this is not an industrial country and there just plain aren't any jobs for these people. You can't take some hundred and twenty-five thousand people off their land in an agricultural province and expect them to make a decent life for themselves around the towns. In the Song Ve Valley operation, for the first time, we got a little bit of Psy War in, so at least the people had a faint idea of what was coming, but that was only because of our insistence. Before that, there was *nothing*. Those people didn't know *why* they were getting kicked out, *where* they were going, or *what* was going to happen to them. You wouldn't believe the contradictions in the situation here. If I told people about this back in the States, they'd say I was lying. And every situation is different. No two camps are the same and no two operations are the same. And every one is being carried on separately from the others. The Army suddenly just tells us that five thousand people are going to arrive, with no possessions and no food. It's like a band where everybody's trying to play a solo at the same time—you know what kind of music that makes."

Later, I saw one of the Psychological Warfare leaflets that had been dropped over the Song Ve Valley. On one side is a photograph of a man and his wife, each holding a small boy. All four members of the family are smiling at the camera. The caption reads, "I, Trinh Su, and my family have resettled in the Nghia Hanh resettlement camp, where we have received sufficient aid from the G.V.N. I advise you to follow instructions of the U.S. Army in Nghia Hanh and you will live in safety, as we do." On the back, the text reads:

> People of the Song Ve Valley, the G.V.N. urges those of you that are still living in the mountains to come down and move to Nghia Hanh. There you will be protected and cared for by the G.V.N. and Allied Forces. Your friends who have moved to Nghia Hanh have received food and medical care. At Nghia Hanh you will be safe. There will be shelter for you and your family. Those of you who choose to remain in the area will be considered hostile and in danger.

Eventually, I talked with one of the men who took photographs for such leaflets. He was an American private about six feet four inches tall and very stout. "We make funny faces and kind of horse around to get them to laugh or smile," he told me. "We were trying to get one old buzzard about sixty years old to laugh, but he just stood there without cracking a smile, no matter what we did. But then I was climbing up a stepladder to shoot a picture, and I kind of slipped and fell off it, and you should have seen the old bastard laugh then!"

Before I left Mr. Hobson, he explained to me that one of his greatest problems was finding out which foods were suitable for preparation in the camps. After rice, the principal staple in the American relief supply was bulgur wheat. Mr. Hobson had discovered, however, that the people in the camps, even when they were hungry, sold the wheat to pig farmers—partly because they disliked the taste of wheat gruel but mainly because it took too much firewood to cook the wheat. There was a great scarcity of firewood, particularly in the camps, and to use several days' supply of grass and twigs to prepare one meal of bulgur wheat spelled hunger as surely as using up a week's supply of rice in one day. Mr. Hobson said, "It's hard for us Americans to tell what is good for the Vietnamese. For instance, it's hard to tell the difference between a rich man and a poor man. They don't have any washing machines or fancy houses. The difference might just be a motor scooter out front. So to the G.I.s everyone looks poor."

Mr. Hobson credited his continuing education in Vietnamese customs to his assistant, a Mr. Te, for whom he expressed high respect. "Mr. Te is going to make a real Vietnamese gentleman out of me someday," he said, half to me, half to Mr. Te. "And the first thing that's got to go is my loud laugh. I've got a loud laugh, and Mr. Te says that's the No. 1 problem. But I've got to be myself, so I'll have to become a gentleman *with* my loud laugh." He gave his loud laugh.

Later in our talk, he said, "I ask you, if we can't win the allegiance of a captive audience in these camps, how are we going to win their hearts and minds out in a hamlet way off in the boonies somewhere? The big shots want to move everyone all around. They say, 'The Montagnards gotta learn to live in the lowland, the farmers gotta learn to live in the towns.' The trouble is, they have no heart. They just plain have no heart."

I said I had noticed that statistics on refugees in the province listed tens of thousands of people as having been "resettled."

Mr. Hobson explained that this had all taken place under the "Refugee Relief Operational Handbook" provisions for "Resettlement in Temporary Camps." "All that resettlement is just paperwork," he said. "We're supposed to give each family five thousand p's"—that is, piastres—"as a resettlement housing allowance, so they can build a new house, but what we do is say, 'O.K., this place we've built for you is now *permanent,* it's *yours,* so you don't get the five thousand p's.' Another way of doing it is to put in a village chief and give the camp a *name.* Then it can be treated as a village or a hamlet. Of course, the place has to meet certain criteria, but basically it's paperwork. What it means is that the place goes out of the hands of the Special Commissariat for Refugees and into the hands of the Ministry of Social Welfare—which is *also* me!" Mr. Hobson again gave the laugh that was holding him back from becoming a Vietnamese gentleman. But he quickly became silent, and shook his head. "I don't have time to find out where they're coming from," he said. "All I can do is try to get them some food and put roofs over their heads, because otherwise they haven't got a damn thing going for them."

On October 6th, a British physician who had worked in Quang Ngai's civilian hospital—there is just one in the entire province—for over three years wrote in a report that health conditions in the camps "differ from camp to camp," explaining:

> More established [camps] are a little better.
> They usually have a pseudo nurse, toilet, and
> well. Disease, poverty, and malnutrition com-
> mon.
> New camps: poor water and toilet facilities,
> little money, little food, housing poor, cold,
> and again disease and malnutrition common.
> Recent camps: hovels, no housing, tents,
> camp in the open, no water, no toilets, no
> money, no food, diseases like dysentery, ma-
> laria, malnutrition, infectious hepatitis, plague
> an everyday occurrence. Many people die—
> average 2 to 3 a week—from any of the above
> causes. Now with the rainy season starting
> their immediate future is terrible indeed. Of
> this category there are approximately 5,000–
> 10,000 in the province.

At the beginning of 1967, American officials in Vietnam, both military and civilian, commonly expressed the view that the "generation of refugees" was an unfortunate but unavoidable consequence of conducting effective military operations. By August, most officials were declaring that the removal of people from their original homes and villages was in itself a valuable tactic in the struggle against the National Liberation Front. Military men, in particular, were fond of quoting Mao Tse-tung's dictum that in guerrilla warfare the guerrillas are the fish and the people are the water. They argued that they could catch the fish only by drying up the water. I heard Mao Tse-tung's metaphor mentioned in this connection on at least five occasions in Quang Ngai. In an article titled "The Cause in Vietnam Is Being Won," which appeared in the issue of *The New York Times Magazine* of October 15, 1967, General Maxwell D. Taylor, former chairman of the Joint Chiefs of Staff and former United States Ambassador to South Vietnam, explains the logic of population control and, without naming the camps as such, describes the advantages to the South Vietnamese government of having from three million to four million of the country's population of roughly seventeen million in or around government-controlled camps:

> As an indicator of progress in pacification, there has been an encouraging increase in Government control in rural areas in recent months. Indeed, since mid-1965, there has been an increase of some 3 million people in rural areas clearly under Government control. About 1,200,000 of this increase has occurred in the last six months. Concurrently, the Vietcong-controlled population has decreased by more than a million since 1965, the remaining Governmental gains having come from contested areas. In that year, it was estimated that 26 per cent of the total population (including the cities) was under Vietcong domination; now it is down to 14 per cent. If one includes the cities, the total population under secure Government of Vietnam control has increased from 6.6 million in mid-1965 to 10.8 million in mid-1967. . . .

> Population liberated from Vietcong control
> is a double asset from our point of view. Not
> only are these people freed from the tyranny
> of Vietcong domination, but they are with-
> drawn from among the human assets so neces-
> sary to support the guerrilla movement. The
> Vietcong are necessarily parasitic upon the
> rural population from whom they drew re-
> cruits, porters, food and other forms of help.
> Without this rural support, the local guerrilla
> movement risks atrophy and progressive at-
> trition.

I met a young American lieutenant colonel in Binh Son
District who was discouraged by the current situation in
the province but thought that things would improve
greatly if a sweeping plan he had in mind should be put
into effect. After talking for over a year with Vietnamese
whose command of English was poor, the colonel had
developed a very slow, careful style of enunciation and had
come to employ a minimal basic vocabulary. This way of
speaking had become such a habit with him that at times
he used it even with Americans, especially when he was
trying to elucidate difficult points. His slowness of speech
was accompanied by strong emphasis on every important
word and a tense, passionate gesticulation with his fists that
expressed his total dedication to his work. Sometimes he
would expend so much energy explaining an idea about
the future of the province that he would have to slump
back in his chair with a weak smile of exhaustion when he
had finished.

While I was with the colonel, I heard him tell an
observer from the American headquarters for Pacification
in Saigon, who had come to evaluate the "potential" of the
province for Revolutionary Development, which is the

South Vietnamese government's response to the Vietcong's political-indoctrination program, and is usually abbreviated as revdev, or R.D., "Look, the V.C. get their people to support them. They *organize* the people. Those people are *alive;* they are highly *motivated.* But the people who are supposed to be on our side are just *blobs.*" He screwed up his face in chagrin and clenched his fists in front of him. "The refugees sit around all day doing *nothing,* and *we are doing nothing about it,*" he continued, coming down hard on every word. Then he outlined his plan for reconstruction. "We've got to get these people out where they can get killed," he said, then stopped himself, smiled, and added, "Don't get me wrong. I don't want them to suffer any more than they are suffering now. They've suffered too much already, but what I mean is, we've got to give them some *reason* to support the government. We have to give them some motivation to defend themselves. Now they don't have any jobs, or houses, or anything that they can get excited about, and I don't blame them for being apathetic. Look at the camps. *Anybody* would be apathetic." The first requirement for reconstruction, as he saw it, was security, and for this he envisaged a vast, superbly conducted training program for the local young men, who would learn a new self-confidence and the will to defend their villages against the National Liberation Front. Next, the villages would have to be physically rebuilt—"preferably by the villagers themselves." He said, "The Vietnamese have to do it themselves. We always try to do it for them, to give it to them. I know what a tremendous temptation it is to give candy to kids. It makes you feel good inside. You're No. 1. But for every piece of candy you give a kid, you're destroying the kid's faith in his father, who can't give him any candy. I have seen so many cases of Americans who want to play Santa Claus and feel warm all over, but this kind of thing is only corrupting, and it destroys the people's pride. If only we could learn that!" The next part of the plan involved the creation of a democratic village government, chosen by the people themselves and responsive to their aspirations. Finally, the change at the local level would be accompanied by the total abolition of corruption at the provincial level, and the beginnings of a nationwide changeover to civilian rule. In short, the colonel wanted to see a vigorous, democratic, prosperous, happy, entirely new and changed society rise from the ashes of Quang Ngai to resist the National Liberation Front because the local villagers felt a spontaneous love for their new life and a deep enthusiasm for a wholly reformed government of South Vietnam.

I pointed out to the colonel that approximately seventy per cent of the villages in the province had already been destroyed, and asked if he saw this as a serious obstacle to the realization of his plan.

"I know it," he said. "In the fifteen-kilometre stretch of coast of our area of operation there are just *two* villages still standing, and if anyone tells you there are more they are liars. One thing is that the Vietnamese can rebuild their houses very quickly, with very little trouble at all." He then patiently described to me in detail how the thatch-roofed houses that had made up about eighty per cent of the homes in the province were constructed. "The thing is, we've got to change the population patterns," he went on. "It's these widely dispersed *population patterns* that allowed the V.C. to get going in the first place. So we won't necessarily move the people back to their original villages. If we could change the population patterns, getting people consolidated into tighter areas, we could put up defenses, and the government could control them more easily. We could check them every night for I.D. cards, and in that way keep the V.C. from infiltrating.''

When the colonel had concluded his remarks, the observer from Saigon said that he would like to spend a day and a night in a village of the district with his Vietnamese interpreter, to judge for himself whether conditions were ripe for a Revolutionary Development Program, and he asked the colonel to recommend a village. Clapping a hand to his forehead, the colonel laughed in dismay, and said, "You can't sleep in a village. I couldn't let you do that. We don't have any villages an *American* could spend the *night* in."

After completing Operation Malheur II in the Song Ve Valley, the 1st Brigade of the 101st Airborne Division took another hop in its drive northward and launched Operation Hood River in the Song Tra Khuc Valley. The hope was to trap a large unit of the enemy by landing on the hills above the valley and sweeping down into it from all sides, but, as in the two earlier operations, the trap closed empty. Sporadic contact with the enemy was common during these sweeps, but this time it was lighter than usual. The official figure for enemy killed during the two weeks of the operation was seventy-eight, and the figure for American casualties was three killed and thirty-eight wounded. The troops, and the artillery and aircraft that supported them, did, however, destroy most of the villages in the river valley and on the coastal plain at its mouth.

In mid-August, when I first arrived at the Chu Lai base,

which is situated just north of Quang Ngai Province, in the southern part of Quang Tin Province, and which was the headquarters for Task Force Oregon at that time, I was given a briefing on the composition of the enemy in Quang Ngai Province by the head Information Officer for the task force, Major Patrick H. Dionne, who is a portly man with a round face and a smile that appears, along with an outstretched hand, as soon as someone enters his office— a greeting that seems to say, "We're going to get along fine!" (Throughout my stay in Quang Ngai, I was given perfect freedom to see whatever I wanted, and was encouraged by Major Dionne and other Information Officers to fly in FAC planes and accompany operations on the ground as often as possible.)

"We're here to sell the government of South Vietnam to the people in this province," Major Dionne said. "The trouble is, they don't *want* to have the government sold to them, so what we are really doing is cramming the government down their throats. This place has been V.C. ever since the Japanese, so they've never really had any contact with the government." Picking a pink card out of a desk file for reference, he continued, "There are from seven hundred thousand to a million people in Quang Ngai. About half of these are under G.V.N. control and a quarter are V.C. supporters. We've got quite a large number of refugees in the province. They fled the V.C. or left their area because of combat, and now the G.V.N. controls them. We've got both local V.C. and N.V.A. units in the province. The 3rd N.V.A. Division is based in Duc Pho District."

I asked if these North Vietnamese Army soldiers had infiltrated into South Vietnam recently.

"Actually, these are the ones that came down in 1954 and stayed, and they organized the local people to support

Hanoi," Major Dionne said. "You might say that the people are North Vietnamese–oriented—living on this side of the D.M.Z. The N.V.A. here are the old Vietminh who stayed on. They have their families down here and don't really have too much to go back to up North. Then, there's the V.C.—the local-force guy and the main-force guy. The local-force guy lives at home and is poorly armed—a squad might have two rifles and six hand grenades—but he's highly motivated, and does the political cadre work. As opposed to the N.V.A., the local V.C. is a loner—with a lot of other loners. They feel pretty sure that they are going to succeed. The main-force guy is organized in units and roves around. He's better armed."

When I spoke with American officers about the civilians who were sometimes killed in our bombings of villages judged to be hostile, they often brought up the fact that the Vietcong also mistreated and killed civilians in *their* operations. During my month in Quang Ngai Province, two incidents of this kind figured heavily in Army press releases, in battalion newspapers, and in Psychological Warfare posters and leaflets. On August 9th, the Vietcong had attacked a village along Route 1 that was supposed to be protected by Popular Forces stationed there. The Popular Forces had fired at the Vietcong, but without venturing outside their fortified positions, and the Vietcong had destroyed a dozen houses with satchel charges and killed and wounded several villagers; they had, however, left the medical dispensary, which was financially supported by Americans, untouched. Army photographers arrived the next morning to take photographs of civilians wounded or killed in the attack. Later, these photographs were printed on propaganda posters and were also released to the press. The other incident was the discovery of two men that the Vietcong had held prisoner for several months. The August 16th edition of the *Screaming Eagle* reported the discovery as follows:

> Duc Pho—"God, they were a mess," said one paratrooper. "They looked like something out of those World War II prison camps." The 101st Airborne trooper was shocked at the physical condition of two South Vietnamese soldiers liberated from a Viet Cong prison camp near here during Operation Malheur II. The prisoners were emaciated, haggard and beaten. Eyes and cheeks were sunk into their gaunt faces and their voices weak and inaudible due to lack of strength. Both suffered from malnutrition and exhaustion.
>
> "They were in pretty bad shape," said Lt. Corky Boswell, Chico, Calif. "The VC had beaten them, used them for laborers, and fed them just enough to keep them alive. And that wasn't very much, as you can see. . . ." The two former prisoners, exhausted, and limited in their knowledge of enemy movements, were of little help. "We can't help you," said Xuan.
>
> "We just dug tunnels. They watched us carefully all the time and never talked in front of us."

Major Dionne expressed deep disgust with the Vietcong for attacking the village on Route 1. "O.K., so maybe one of our artillery rounds goes astray and hits a friendly village every once in a while," he said. "But I don't know." Major Dionne's expression became disturbed. "With a hidden device—a V.C. mine . . . I mean, *I* get paid to wear the uniform, so if something happens to me it's not so bad. But these poor old buzzards don't get paid for that. I don't know . . ."

Every few weeks or so, the Vietcong overran another village along Route 1 that was supposed to be under the protection of the Popular Forces. In October, I asked U.S. AID officials in Washington how many village officials had been assassinated by the Vietcong in 1967 in Quang Ngai Province. When AID or any other government agency gives statistics on "village officials" killed, these may include officers of the Popular Forces and members of the Combat Youth—these are both lightly armed groups of villagers recruited to defend their own villages against the Vietcong—and Revolutionary Development workers, Civic Action cadres, interfamily chiefs, security agents, and a great variety of other types of individuals. For the period from January 1st to October 1st, AID listed a total of eighteen "village officials" as having been killed by the Vietcong in Quang Ngai. They consisted of three Revolutionary Development workers, three hamlet chiefs, two Youth Cadre members, one Civic Action cadre, four Popular Forces officers, one Combat Youth member, one chief of a rehabilitation center, one former village security agent, one village security agent, and one former interfamily chief. Usually, the Vietcong were careful to bomb only the houses of government employees, and several Americans expressed horror at the coldblooded premeditation of these assassinations. "We may have accidents," said one, "but we never set off a mine or shoot a bullet with some specific guy's name written on it in advance."

Major Dionne told me that Task Force Oregon's proudest nonmilitary achievement was the opening of Route 1 to traffic. When the task force arrived, it found that the Vietcong had blown up almost all the bridges on the road. Task Force Oregon engineers rebuilt the bridges and then opened the road to public traffic in a big ceremony, with several high-ranking officers of Task Force

Oregon and the province chief present. Several times each week, American teams swept the road for Vietcong mines, finding an average of two a week. A light traffic of bicycles and motor scooters began to travel between certain towns, although other stretches were still unused.

Later on, Major Dionne told me, "When I get to wondering what this war is all about, I take a trip up to the base hospital. You know—a guy smilin' at you, saying that he's going to be up in a few weeks, when what he doesn't know is that he's lost the use of his legs and is crippled for life. And when I see what these boys are willing to sacrifice, that really makes me see what it's all about over here."

I also spoke briefly with an Intelligence captain assigned to the FAC control desk about the character of the enemy. "They have a parallel structure," he told me. "The orders originate in Hanoi and go to COSVN." He pronounced it "Cosvin" and explained that it meant the Central Office of South Vietnam.

I asked if he would tell me what he meant by a parallel structure.

"O.K., let's take a look at Communism—at North Vietnam, the U.S.S.R., and China," he said. "They all have a front organization that tells the people that the government has moral objectives that are sound. All these countries have that in common."

"What does the front organization consist of?" I asked.

"It's the fact that they have a President."

"How does this apply to the National Liberation Front?"

"I don't know precisely how the front and the real government are related, but the front is the organization that tries to tell them that Communism is a good deal."

"If there is a parallel structure, what is parallel to what?" I asked.

"The Front is one—the National Liberation Front—and

the other . . . Oh, hell, I can't think of the other. Did you read Allen Dulles' book about intelligence?"

I said I hadn't.

"It's described in there. There's the apparatus that spreads Communism. But I forget what they call it here." (That night, the captain came in to tell me he had done some research and had found the name that had eluded him earlier—it was the People's Revolutionary Party.)

Conversations in Vietnam tend to become muddled because many meanings are attached to a few favorite terms, as in the above conversation, in which the Intelligence captain often failed to make it clear when we meant "front" in the sense of the National Liberation Front and when we meant it in the sense of a cover, or front, organization. Later, I was talking with the same captain about "the V.C. infrastructure," and I suddenly realized that this term, which he had used at the beginning of the conversation to mean the political organization of the Vietcong at the local level, had changed as we talked to mean the wood-and-packed-mud "infrastructure" of the Vietcong's tunnels and bunkers. "Parallel structure" is another of the favorite terms, and it can apply to the Vietcong governmental apparatus, which "parallels" the South Vietnamese government, or to the American advisory system, which also "parallels" the South Vietnamese government, or, as in my conversation with the captain, to the "parallel structure" of all Communist governments, including the National Liberation Front. (The word "structure" is itself a favorite in Vietnam. The military refer to all Vietnamese houses as "structures.")

After completing Operation Hood River, the 1st Brigade of the 101st Airborne Division was to move north once again and launch Operation Benton, in the southern part of Quang Tin Province. I flew over the Song Tra Khuc Valley in FAC planes—assigned by the Air Force to the 1st Brigade of the 101st Airborne Division—during the last two days of Operation Hood River. FAC pilots had two duties. The first was to fly over specified areas noting anything that seemed suspicious to them and choosing targets to recommend for air strikes. The targets were not further examined at first hand, and unless they were found to be near friendly troops or in "no-strike zones" they were bombed. Some FAC pilots flew over a certain area every day for several weeks at a time, acquainting themselves with it as thoroughly as they could from the air with the aid of maps. Other pilots would be assigned to the brigade, and would fly over the brigade in all its operations, wherever it went. The FAC pilots' second duty was to guide fighter-bombers to their targets. Air Force spokesmen were always careful to stress the point that a FAC pilot could not, on his own authority, call planes to bomb a target—that the Army had to give its clearance in every case. In practice, this meant that when a FAC pilot spotted something he wished to have bombed he would radio its position to the DASC (Direct Air Support Center) office for his military corps area and enter a request for a flight of fighter-bombers. DASC would weigh the urgency of the mission against other requests made for fighter-bombers at that particular time, and decide which of the requested targets should be bombed by the limited number of planes that were aloft or "on hot pad alert," ready for immediate takeoff. The Air Force divided all air strikes into two categories, which it termed "pre-planned strikes" and "immediate strikes." A pre-planned strike was scheduled anywhere from twenty-four hours to two weeks in advance of the time of the bombing, and an immediate strike was carried out within a few hours, at most, of a call from ground troops or from a FAC pilot who had spotted what he judged to be enemy activity. In conversation with a FAC pilot, I once said "planned strike" instead of "pre-planned strike," by mistake, and was swiftly corrected. When I asked what the difference between the terms "planned" and "pre-planned" was, the pilot answered, "*All* our strikes are *planned*. We *have* no *unplanned* strikes."

At the Danang airbase, I received a briefing from a major on the role of FAC pilots in I Corps. When I asked what kinds of targets were usually hit by pre-planned strikes, he answered, "In the mountains, just about anything that moves is considered to be V.C. We've cleared most of the people out of there, and anything that's left has got to be V.C. No one else has got any reason to be there. We go after enemy base areas and V.C. r.-and-r. centers." The Army refers to the overnight way stations where Vietcong soldiers are believed to sleep as "r.-and-r. centers," after the Army's own practice of sending its troops for one week of "rest and relaxation" each year in a foreign capital, like Bangkok, Tokyo, or Sydney. "Most of the action is in the lowlands," the major continued. "There we hit mostly the bunkers and fortifications. The V.C. hide in there, and store their supplies in there, too. Of course, we can never hit *all* the bunkers. Also, we hit fortified villages. In some of these villages, the lines of trenches and bunkers are amazing. It looks like World

War I. These fortified villages are all known to be enemy installations. I mean, they've been shooting at people and harboring the V.C. But before we hit any place we send a Psy War craft in to warn the villagers to escape. We used to drop warning leaflets, but they didn't do much good, so now we've switched over to announcing. We give the people at least a good ten or fifteen minutes to get out of there before we put in a strike. But it's the immediate strike that gives the best results. That's where you get your K.B.A.s." The initials stand for "Killed by Air." "Of course," the major added, "enemy troops in the open are the kind of target that we all like the best."

I asked him what was involved in getting clearance for an air strike.

"First, we check the area for friendly troops, and then, when the request goes in to DASC, the province chief has to give his O.K.," he said. "We *never* put in a strike without first getting permission from the province chief. He's a Vietnamese, and he knows the local conditions, so he's the man in the final analysis who knows who's friendly and who's unfriendly. And, after all, it's their country, so they ought to know what's going on." (Later, I asked Province Chief Hoang Dinh Tho, of Quang Tin Province, about the specific steps that were usually taken in securing his clearance, and learned that at the beginning of each operation in his province he designated certain regions—typically, those surrounding district capitals—as no-strike zones, and gave the ground commanders of the operation a free hand in deciding which targets to bomb in the rest of the area of operation.)

The major explained that the Vietnam Air Force (or VNAF, pronounced "Veenaf" by the Americans) had its own organization, separate from the United States Air Force but flying out of the same bases. VNAF supported

ARVN with A-1 propeller-driven fighter-bombers—a type of plane that was last used by our Navy in the Korean war. "VNAF has its own FACS," the major told me. "They work just the way we do. One-half of the base is for VNAF and one-half for us."

I asked what VNAF FACS did, mostly.

"VNAF FACS usually cover convoys," the major replied. "They're pretty much tied up with that. But it's a very necessary function—to cover those convoys. VNAF uses one side of Danang. We built the facilities just the same as the American facilities, but separate. But they don't know how to take care of something nice. You go over there now, and it's a stinking mess. You know what one of the first things they did was? They unscrewed the taps and spigots in the bathrooms and took them into town and sold them."

I asked whether American FACS guided the VNAF fighter-bombers to their targets.

"Those old A-1s that VNAF uses are a lot slower than our planes, and more accurate, so they don't use any FACS for that," the major answered.

I learned that ideas for targets of the American fighter-bombers were gathered mainly from the recommendations of ground commanders, FAC pilots, and "agent reports"— the name given to most other sources of information. Occasionally, a province chief would order a town burned or bombed. All targets were described to DASC in terms of their coördinates on a military map, and DASC would relay these coördinates to the FAC pilot who was guiding the air strike. The FAC pilot would locate the target point on a similar map that he carried with him in the plane. The maps were crosshatched by a grid. The horizontal lines, spaced two centimetres apart, were numbered from 01 to 99, and the vertical lines were similarly spaced and numbered. Each square formed by the lines represented one square kilometre on the ground. The coördinates were given in six figures divided into two groups of three—691 873, for example. The first two digits of the first group of three designated a vertical line, and the first two digits of the second group of three designated a horizontal line. The third digit of the first group indicated a distance, in hundreds of metres, east of the vertical line on the map, and the third digit of the second group indicated a distance, in hundreds of metres, north of the horizontal line. However, the hundred-metre intervals were not drawn on the map, so the pilot had to estimate for himself what one hundred, or three hundred, metres along the lines amounted to. And even if the pilot estimated accurately, the smallest area that could be designated by this system was a hundred metres square. (Everything within the hundred-metre square northeast of the coördinates 691 873 was designated by those coördinates.) On about half the missions, DASC would give the FAC pilot a description of the type of target that was to be located in the hundred-metre-square area designated by the coördinates. Some of the official descriptions, such as "bunkers," "military structures," and "enemy hamlet," referred to targets that could sometimes be spotted from the air, but other descriptions, such as "V.C. r.-and-r. area," "suspected enemy troop concentration," and "infiltration route" did not, and in these cases the pilot had to rely entirely on his coördinates. Once the pilot had found the target area on his map, he would plot its position on the ground by using as reference points prominent topographical features that showed on his map; in the mountains he would use the configurations of the ridgelines as reference points, and in the flatlands he would use rivers, roads, and villages. After finding the target on the ground, he would relay the coördinates by radio to the fighter-bombers when they came overhead.

Just before the strike, he would "mark" the target by hitting it with a phosphorus rocket, which sends up a highly visible cloud of white smoke and also splashes burning phosphorus over a twenty-yard area. Then, using the smoke as a guide, the fighter-bombers would fly over the target, dropping their bombs or cans of napalm, or hitting it with rockets or strafing fire. The FAC plane meanwhile circled slowly nearby, watching the strike and telling the pilots of the fighter-bombers by radio how far from the target they were hitting. Usually, there were two or three fighter-bomber planes on a mission, and each plane flew two or three passes, depending on what armament it was carrying. When the strike was completed, the FAC pilot would fly over the area again and make a Bomb Damage Assessment Report—usually called the B.D.A. Report—to DASC and to the fighter-bomber pilots. The B.D.A. Report included the percentage of "Bombs on Target" and the percentage of "Target Destroyed." The pilot would also report any "Military Structures Destroyed." When there were friendly ground troops in the area near the target, the ground commander would radio the coördinates of their position to the FAC pilot, who would relay the information to the pilots of the fighter-bombers. The FAC pilot would make contact with the commanders of nearby artillery batteries, too, to check the trajectory of artillery shells being fired at that moment, so that he would be able to avoid them. A FAC pilot told me that one in twenty FAC pilots was killed during 1966, but he explained that he and his fellow-pilots felt less fear than many G.I.s on the ground who had a smaller chance of being hit. In the air, you didn't know when you were being shot at until a bullet came very close to the plane, or actually hit it, the pilot said, and he described a bullet passing close by as making a snapping sound, "like someone closing an ashtray in the back seat of your car." The fighter-bomber pilots made no decisions about targets themselves. A fighter-bomber pilot who was based at Danang told me, "We are going four or five hundred knots, and we can't see much ourselves. I've never seen a body or a person yet, and I've been on over a hundred missions. It's virtually impossible to see any movement on the ground. The FAC is the expert. We're only experts on delivery."

In August, there were six FAC pilots detailed to the 1st Brigade of the 101st Airborne Division. During Operations Malheur I and Malheur II, they had flown out of Duc Pho, but as the brigade moved north for Operation Hood River and Operation Benton, the FAC pilots shifted their base of operation north to Chu Lai. While the brigade was conducting an operation, the FAC pilots always kept one plane aloft over the area of operation during daylight hours. Each pilot usually flew a three-hour shift each day, though occasionally, when an emergency called for it, each would fly a six-hour shift. From August 10th to August 21st, I flew with the FAC pilots attached to the 1st of the 101st almost daily, lived with them in their quarters, and ate my meals with them on the base.

On August 10th, the next-to-last day of Operation Hood River, I flew in the early morning with a FAC pilot from Texas who had a thin face and a slight frame and was about thirty years old. I shall call him Captain Reese. The standard FAC plane was a Cessna O-1 Bird Dog. It seated two, one in front and one in back; had a single propeller; and was armed with four tubes containing phosphorus rockets, two tubes being mounted under each wing. It could fly as slowly as forty miles an hour, and could hold an extremely tight corkscrew turn when the pilot wanted to look at one small area of ground for a sustained period.

Before climbing into the plane, Captain Reese picked up a flak vest, a helmet, a submachine gun, and a survival kit, the last two for use in case the plane was hit and had to make a forced landing. On the flight line, where the planes sat enclosed by steel walls to protect them from shrapnel in mortar or rocket attacks, three young mechanics lounged shirtless in the heat, waiting to refuel O-1 planes or repair their engines. Although it was against the rules, the pilots occasionally let the mechanics climb into the pilot's seat and taxi the planes across the fifty-yard stretch of asphalt between the fuel pump and the protective walls.

Just before our plane went out on the runway, one of the mechanics, who was pulling safety rods from the rocket tubes on the wings, asked Captain Reese, "You gonna get any of 'em today, Captain?"

"I dunno," answered Captain Reese.

The mechanics often asked the pilots about their missions, but they rarely got answers any more revealing than this. During most of the day, the mechanics sat on wooden boxes around a soft-drink cooler that was protected by a canvas roof, and read back issues of *Stars and Stripes,* or looked for the hundredth time through a few thumb-greased copies of *Sir!* and *Escapade* magazines. Beyond their little spot of shade stretched a landscape of hot asphalt, shimmering corrugated metal, and airplanes. Part of their job was to assemble phosphorus rockets and load them under the wings of the FAC planes. The rockets were about a yard long and came in three pieces, which the mechanics had to screw together. I once asked a mechanic who had just dumped a case of four rockets on the asphalt whether a rocket would explode if he tossed it up in the air and let it fall onto the runway. He picked up a front section, which was marked "Warhead," and, dangling it about five feet off the ground, said, "It would go off if I dropped it from here. If it gets on you, it'll burn right through you for days and it won't go out with just water. You have to put it out with a special chemical we've got over there in the shed." The mechanics did not learn about any military operation that the FAC planes supported until four or five days after it had been launched, when a copy of the Task Force Oregon mimeographed *News Sheet* might reach them, and they could read, for example, "The infantry units mounted a three-pronged attack, and in the ensuing ground action tallied 44 enemy killed, bringing the body count to 65 for the action north of Duc Pho," or "Two Chinese mines were discovered by the airborne-infantrymen as they searched for the enemy in heavy jungle west of Quang Ngai City. One detainee, suffering a bullet wound in the back, was turned over to authorities. The paratroopers captured three enemy weapons and one and one-half tons of rice." Every once in a while, one of the mechanics would get a word or two out of a FAC pilot about a current operation, and he would relay the information to the other mechanics with studied nonchalance, as though he always had an inside line on what was going on. But usually the mechanics just fuelled the planes, watched them disappear in the sky, read old magazines, and listened to the day-long thunder of bombs on the other side of the mountains.

When Captain Reese and I had strapped ourselves into our seats, a young mechanic waved us forward onto a siding of the runway. Captain Reese had to wait for an F-4 fighter-bomber to take off ahead of us. The F-4 was mottled with green and brown camouflage paint and had a heavy, sharklike body with stubby wings, downward-slanting tail fins, and a drooping black nose, which was just rising off the runway as the plane crossed our bow. For a few seconds, the deep roaring of its engine filled one's head completely, overpowering thought. In a quarter of a minute, the orange-tipped blue flames of its afterburners were vanishing in the distance as it rose at a steady steep angle.

Captain Reese taxied onto the runway, and our small plane lifted off the asphalt after running only a hundred yards or so down the runway, which was two miles long and stretched out of sight in front of us like a turnpike in a desert. As soon as the plane was off the ground, Captain Reese turned southwest and started a climb to fifteen hundred feet. According to regulations, the FAC pilots were not supposed to fly below that altitude, but almost all of them frequently broke this rule, and sometimes they went down as low as a hundred feet. ("As soon as I heard that rule, I knew that it was one of the rules made to break," a FAC pilot once said to me. "You can't even see people from one thousand feet. You can't see anything unless you go down there.") Captain Reese guided the O-1 over the brown, abandoned rice fields and blackened ruins of the villages in the western part of Son Tinh District. There was a heavy, high gray overcast.

Using a headset and a microphone wired for the back seat, I asked Captain Reese what types of target were most common and what the targets of the present mission were.

Speaking through a microphone the size of a lima bean that reached around on a small metal arm from the side of his helmet almost into his mouth, Captain Reese answered, "Oh, usually we get a V.C. base camp, burn off a village, or hit a supply depot. Today, we're going to hit a suspected enemy troop concentration at 324 733." (All figures given for coördinates in this account have been changed.)

I asked how it had been decided to bomb this target.

"I don't know. An agent reported it, or something, I guess," he said.

We crossed a small ridge of hills and came out over the Song Tra Khuc Valley. The cultivated fields were pale green, and the forests on the mountain slopes were a vivid deep green under a sky that was darkening before rain. Several miles to the west, where the valley vanished into the mountains, curved plumes of rain trailed down from the cloud cover, and to the east more plumes of rain descended into the sea. The air below the clouds seemed oddly clear, and tall, bluish mountains were visible far to the west, above the delicate ridges of nearer, smaller mountains. The line between the sea and the sky was lost in a uniform grayness, and a large blue island, clearly visible twenty or more kilometres offshore, seemed to be floating in the sky. The tops of four or five of the low mountains on the north and south sides of the valley were bald and blackened. Captain Reese explained that intensive bombing and machine-gun fire were usually directed at hilltops—often starting forest fires—in order to kill anyone there before our troops made a landing. In the valley, the cultivated fields were marked with craters of all sizes. Five or six thin, straight columns of smoke rose from the valley floor. "They're burning off some hootches. This is a solid V.C. area," Captain Reese told me. He circled lower, for a closer look. In that part of the valley, widely separated clusters of houses stood along a line of trees bordering a small stream. Troops were advancing across a rice field and entering a courtyard that was surrounded by three houses. A minute later, as they reappeared in a field on the other side of the yard, a spot of flame began to spread on the roof of one house, then on the roof of another, and soon all three roofs were collapsing in flames. Captain Reese brought the plane back to fifteen hundred feet and headed southwest again, toward his target area. Below us, the gray squares of freshly burned houses dotted the ground. Arriving over the target area, Captain Reese found that the hundred-metre square designated by the coördinates included a wooded ridge and a small ravine lying halfway up a mountain about three thousand feet high. The side of the ravine across from the ridge was lined with rows of crops stretching up the steep mountain slope.

"They want us to hit that ravine," Captain Reese said. "That's the target."

At eight-forty-five, the flight commander of three F-4 fighter-bombers radioed to say that they had arrived over the general area.

"Tell me what ordnance you've got, and all that jazz," the Captain said.

"We've got six napes, six seven-hundred-and-fifty-pounders, and six two-hundred-and-fifty pounders. Can you use it?" the flight commander answered.

"We can use all that. I'll mark the target for you," the Captain replied.

Throughout most of the strike, the pilots communicated in relaxed, genial voices and with a perfectly flat intonation, which came across the headsets with a nasal, buzzing quality, perhaps because the pilots placed their lips against the tiny microphones as they talked. Captain Reese spotted the three F-4s through the clear roof of the cockpit as they cut under the clouds above us. Wheeling his plane over the target, he went into a sharp dive, and threw a switch to fire a phosphorus rocket from a tube under his wing. The rocket did not fire. "Damn. Won't fire today," he said. He banked around again, brought the plane into another dive, and threw another switch. Once more, the rocket failed to fire. On his next pass, he dropped a smoke grenade by hand out the window, and it failed to explode. He dropped three more grenades in succeeding passes, and these, too, were duds. The fifth grenade trailed a thin line of smoke from the plane down to the top of the ridge, and a large puff of white smoke soon appeared over the trees. "I want it right down in that valley. You can come in from the east and break west," Captain Reese told the flight commander, and then he began to fly in a tight circle a few hundred yards from the target. As the O-1 was closing its second full circle, he lined up the first fighter-bomber in his front windshield, and he held it in view while it went into a low dive over the cleft. The bombs travelled diagonally earthward and landed on the wooded ridge. A visible shock wave sprang outward from the point of impact, and a cloud of brown smoke shot up several hundred feet above the woods. The fighter-bomber pulled up at a sharp angle, presenting its belly, with the bombs grouped under its stubby wings, to our view. "Real fine!" exclaimed the Captain. "That's right in there! Next time, try to get it fifty metres south, down in the valley." The next plane, diving from the same angle, landed its bombs farther up the ridge. "That's real fine," said the Captain. The third plane sent two silver canisters of napalm toppling down, end over end, and they also landed on the wooded ridge. A pillar of black smoke, with a thick column of orange fire boiling briefly at its core, puffed up over the trees, and red globs of burning jelly splashed outward over the jungle. The next two loads were also napalm, and they also hit the top of the ridge. After the third napalm strike, the flight commander asked, "Do you want it down pretty much in the ravine?" and Captain Reese answered, "Yes, right down there in the ravine." The next three passes put bombs in the ravine, filling it with brown smoke. With that, the strike was over, and the Captain flew back across the target area. Large brown holes had been opened up in the woods, with blasted trees lying in pieces around the edges. Globs of napalm still burned in patches on the ground and in tree branches. At the bottom of the ravine, two bombs had landed directly on a tumbling stream. Above the trees, a flock of birds flying in tight formation wheeled swiftly in circles. One bomb had landed on the cultivated side of the ravine. "I don't see anything," the Captain observed to me, in a tired voice. Then, to the flight commander, he reported, "A hundred per cent of Bombs on Target. Fifty-per-cent Target Coverage. Thank you very much, sir. I've never marked this area before, and I don't seem to mark it very well."

"Not at all," answered the flight commander. Throughout this strike, as in most of the strikes I accompanied, the FAC pilot and the flight commander addressed each other in polite, almost humble tones.

I asked the Captain who had cultivated the fields.

"That's just Montagnard farming. You'd be amazed at the places they farm," he said.

Captain Reese headed the plane back eastward over the Song Tra Khuc Valley. The line of smoking houses along the river was now a kilometre long, and led away from the river into the fields, where two flaming houses marked the troops' advance units. Since the Captain had no further need to talk with the flight commander, he listened in on fragments of conversations on the ground. Communications between ground units crackled into our ears between bursts of static.

"We've captured one Charlie, but we haven't interrogated him yet," said a voice.

"Did he have a weapon?" asked another.

"He had on the black pajamas, short type, but he didn't have a weapon," the first voice replied. "Most likely he hid it somewhere. We found him four hundred metres south of where we were last night."

To me, the Captain said, "Yesterday, five of them ran

into a hole, and came out shooting, and got killed. All the villages around here have foxholes and bunkers under them. This place is almost entirely V.C.-controlled, or pro-V.C."

I asked whether the bunkers did not also serve as bomb shelters for the general populace.

"No," he said. "The V.C. build them—or force the people to build them—strictly for the V.C.'s own protection."

Below us, the lines of smoke from the burning houses had mingled to form a thin haze, which drifted eastward down the valley. DASC at Chu Lai radioed to say that the fighter-bombers assigned to the second target had been diverted to a more urgent mission and would not be coming.

"Well, we'll have to hit it tomorrow, or something," Captain Reese remarked to me.

I took advantage of the lull to ask him about the bombing policy—that is, the policy on the bombing of villages—that he, as a FAC pilot, helped carry out.

"We've got two kinds of strikes—pre-planned and immediate," he answered. "The pre-planned strikes are when we say, 'O.K., you people have been bad now for two or three months, and we haven't been able to talk you into being good, so we're going to wipe you out. You've got twenty-four hours to get out.' Usually, we give them twenty-four hours. That's the pre-planned. Then there's the immediate strike. Now, when there's an Army unit near the village, and they get fire from the village, they say, 'O.K., you people quit shooting or we're going to hit you now—right now.' Of course, that would be in a case where almost everyone in the village is pro-V.C. Technically, the village doesn't have to be warned of a strike when we are flying in conjunction with an operation, like we are now."

While we were talking, we had reached the entrance of the valley, where the river flowed out onto the coastal plain. Here, also, smoke was rising from a roadside, and houses were aflame. The lines of smoke were spreading westward, toward the troops of the 1st Brigade of the 101st, who were moving eastward as they burned more houses. "Those guys down there burning off those hootches are Civilian Irregular Defense Forces," Captain Reese said. "They're Montagnards trained by the Special Forces."

A single main road ran the length of the valley, following the meanderings of the river. Between the villages being burned by the Civilian Irregular Defense Forces and the villages being burned by the 1st Brigade, the road was crowded with cattle and with people carrying double loads on shoulder poles. Near the road, a Special Forces camp had been dug into the bald summit of a round hill that stood alone on the valley floor, overlooking a large village where houses were jammed together inside a small fortified square. Captain Reese said he thought that the village was probably a "new-life" hamlet and would be spared destruction.

As we turned westward again, I asked him about his aerial-reconnaissance duties, and how he distinguished houses and trails used by the enemy from those used only by civilians.

"You look for changes—something that's different," he said. "Normally, you're at fifteen hundred feet, searching for trails and tree lines, and looking for hootches. It's almost a fact that anything out in the open is friendly, so anything you see in the trees you suspect is unfriendly, because it might be V.C. We report hootches that are hidden in tree lines."

I pointed out that, except in the "new-life" hamlets, almost all the houses were built in the shade of tree lines.

"Yeah, they'll be built in the tree lines," he said. "But out in the sticks, if you spot a hootch with no fields around, it's probably V.C. Maybe a rice-storage house."

I asked who lived in the mountains.

"Just the Montagnards and a lot of Vietnamese," he said. "They've taken most of the people out of the mountains, so nobody has any business being here except the V.C. Even the Montagnards here are kind of coöperating with the V.C. We watch for trails up in the mountains, too."

I had noticed that many of the hilltops were cultivated and that most of these were laced with webs of foot trails, and I inquired about the trails.

"I'll look real close at the trails," the Captain said. "If someone walks through one, the grass gets bent."

I asked whether he could spot freshly bent grass from his airplane.

"Oh, yeah, you can tell," he said.

DASC called again, to say that a flight of two fighter-bombers had not expended all its bombs in a previous strike and had been looking for a target for the rest, so DASC had suggested Captain Reese's second target.

To get to the second target, we headed south and crossed a thousand-foot ridge into a small, high abandoned valley, where the rice fields—thickly terraced ones—had already gone wild and the house foundations were half overgrown. Four straight, mile-long avenues of craters from B-52 strikes crisscrossed the valley. The path of craters from one strike began on the ridge on the north side of the valley and marched across the fields and a stream, straight up the southern hillside, and out of sight beyond. The coördinates described a hundred-metre square in a wide stretch of woods on the southern hillside. "We're going to hit a place the troops were in a week ago," Captain Reese said.

"They found some hootches and burned them off. Then, yesterday morning, a FAC pilot spotted some smoke comin' out of there. There wasn't supposed to be any smoke comin' out of there, so we're going to hit it today." Then, looking at his control panel, he exclaimed, "Hell, I forgot to pull the safety switch on the rockets! *That's* why they wouldn't fire." He went on, "You can see that they've hit this target before." He indicated scores of bomb craters and irregular splashes of brown and black from napalm strikes that scarred the woods in the target area. "It's a V.C. base area," he said. "It's got a number. All the base areas have got numbers."

The fighter-bombers for the second strike arrived over the valley and radioed that, all told, they were carrying six five-hundred-pound bombs and four tubes of rockets, with nineteen to a tube. Captain Reese brought the O-1 into a dive, and there was a sharp metallic explosion as a phosphorus rocket fired off our right wing. This was followed by the appearance of a pillar of white smoke rising from the woods. The Captain instructed the flight commander that the F-4s should land their bombs forty metres west of the smoke. Two bombs sent down in the first pass hit a hundred metres east of the smoke. The bombs sent down in the second pass landed fifty metres east, and in the third, and final, bombing pass the bombs landed within thirty metres of the white smoke. The strike continued with four volleys of rockets. Each volley spread over sixty or seventy metres of the woods, sending up puffs of brown smoke, and the rockets were all on the target or within thirty metres of it. Afterward, Captain Reese guided the O-1 into a descending tight spiral over the bomb craters to observe the damage. At the edge of one hole in the woods he saw a pile of debris that he judged to be the remains of a hut, and in his Bomb Damage Assessment Report he mentioned one

"Military Structure Destroyed." At eleven o'clock, he headed our plane back to Chu Lai.

The Chu Lai base had expanded steadily since it was founded, in 1965, and by August of 1967 it was about ten miles long and five miles wide, and occupied what must be one of the world's most beautiful stretches of coastline. A wide beach of pure-white sand runs the length of the base in a gently curving crescent, and the water of the South China Sea is a bluish green, even on cloudy days. Along parts of the shore, a warm surf rolls evenly toward the beach across long sandbars; a mountain island lies off the coast. The area occupied by the base had once been heavily populated. A three-mile-long hilly promontory forming the northern tip of the base had been the site of a dense conglomeration of fishing villages. As the base expanded, leaflets were dropped on these villages announcing that they were going to be destroyed in order to make room for the base. (In the catalogue of leaflets used by the Marines and Task Force Oregon I saw several leaflets of this kind.) The people were evacuated, the villages were bulldozed away, and the Americans laid out their installations on the stretch of bare earth.

Upon landing, Captain Reese started back to headquarters in a jeep. The twenty-minute drive from the FAC flight line to the Task Force Oregon headquarters led through several miles of bulldozed fields of sand and dirt dotted with warehouses, munitions dumps, and repair sheds, and then ran along the beach for a mile or so. The sky was still overcast, and the beach was empty. Beer cans were strewn on the sand around simple canvas roofs on pole frames, which served as canopies for evening cook-outs. (When the sun was out, the waves were usually dotted with heads and with men riding the surf on air mattresses, and the beach was usually covered with suntanned soldiers in bright-colored boxer-style bathing trunks.) Beyond the beach, the road continued up a hill and out onto the rocky promontory at the northern tip of the base. At the top of the promontory, Captain Reese turned right and drove into the command complex of Task Force Oregon. In the center of a dirt parade ground that was surrounded by low, tin-roofed barracks, the American flag and the South Vietnamese flag (three horizontal red stripes on a yellow ground) flew at exactly the same height on two flagpoles standing side by side. Two gaily painted Buddhist shrines, each about ten feet tall and adorned with Chinese characters, also stood on the parade ground. These were the only traces of the Vietnamese villages that had once stood on the site of the base.

Captain Reese had a light lunch and then went to his quarters for a long nap. At just about any time of day after eleven in the morning, two or three of the six pilots could be found sprawled on their beds, asleep in the breeze of an electric fan. The pilots took turns standing by at a central control desk, which was in one of the barracks on the parade ground. It was in constant communication with DASC and with the FAC pilot who was aloft. Although the FAC pilots almost never flew after dark, one of their number helped supervise, from the central control desk, any bombings carried out at night, and coördinated night flights of AC-47s (this was the military version of the DC-3, and was nicknamed Spooky) that supported troops on the ground with heavy fire. On nights when the fighting on the ground was particularly intense, a pilot would have to stay up all night at the control desk and sleep the next day.

Except when the FAC pilots were flying missions, they lived entirely within the confines of their base. It would have been perfectly possible for any one of them to pass his entire one-year tour of duty in Vietnam without ever talking to a Vietnamese or setting foot inside a Vietnamese village or city other than Saigon. Except for their r.-and-r. trips to foreign cities, and occasional expeditions in the FAC planes to the Danang airbase to buy beer and soft drinks, on what they called "the soda-pop run," the pilots' daily lives revolved solely around their missions, their quarters, the central control desk, and the dining halls, bars, and movie theatres in the officers' clubs. The FAC pilots' quarters, which they called the Hootch, consisted of one of the several rows of tin-roofed barracks, which had mosquito netting serving as the upper half of the walls. The barracks was partitioned into three rooms, containing four beds each, and the beds were separated by tall metal clothes cabinets. Most of the pilots had decorated their walls with *Playboy* Playmates of the Month. On the wall next to one major's bed, Miss May of 1967, who is shown standing on a sun deck with her pink shirt open, dwarfed a dozen small snapshots of the major's wife, in one of which she was standing, arms akimbo, in a bathing suit on a beach, and of his eight-year-old son, shown standing beside a lake and holding a small fish up to the camera. On the major's desk were a can of spray insecticide, a Reader's Digest volume of condensed books (featuring President Eisenhower's book "At Ease," which is subtitled "Stories I Tell to Friends"), a can of Pepsi-Cola, a softball, a dozen loose bullets, and a life-size wooden carving of a fist with the middle finger upraised. The Vietnamese do not use the gesture of raising the middle finger, and this kind of sculpture had been developed especially for American soldiers looking for souvenirs of Vietnam. Sometimes the younger pilots played darts on a board that hung on one door, and they also occasionally played Monopoly. A refrigerator was kept stocked with beer and soft drinks.

Because of the heat, most of the pilots had at least two beers or soft drinks a day. Each was on his honor to put fifteen cents in a common refreshment fund in a box in the back of the refrigerator every time he took a drink, but someone who, it seemed, had not been wholly able to put his trust in an honor system had halfheartedly attempted to revise it by taping to the front of the refrigerator door a sheet of paper with everyone's name on it, on which each person was supposed to mark down the number of drinks he had taken and the number he had paid for.

Around the central control desk, and in other places where the pilots gathered, an atmosphere of perpetual low-keyed, comradely humor prevailed. There was a steady stream of light remarks. One man who was standing idly around said to another, with weary joviality, "It's a beautiful, beautiful war!" The second man said, "It's the only one we've got." A FAC pilot entered a room full of FAC pilots and said, "Here are our hard-working FAC pilots," in a tone that indicated neither that they were hard-working nor that they weren't. In this way, the FAC pilots rarely talked about the war directly, and yet never quite got away from the subject, either. The relaxed style of their humor was, I thought, caught quite precisely in their choice as their squadron's emblem of Charles Schulz's comic-strip dog Snoopy, who daydreams of fame as a First World War flying ace. On the outside of the door of the central-control-desk office, Snoopy was depicted, in a sketch, wearing goggles and a scarf that trailed out behind him as he went into a dive in a First World War Sopwith Camel biplane. Cartoon bombs exploded below him. (On a wall of the Duc Pho central-control-desk office, there was a large painting of Snoopy accompanied by a speech balloon that had him saying "Curse you, Charlie Cong!" The Task Force Oregon *News Sheet* reproduced one episode about

Snoopy in each of its issues, and the pilots of the 20th Tactical Air Support Squadron in Danang carried calling cards that depicted Snoopy in his biplane firing a machine gun. On a wall of the squadron's office was a large color poster that bore a reproduction of a painting of an American pilot walking sadly through a prisoner-of-war camp. A vow not to give the enemy any information that was not required by international law was printed below the picture. The pilots, who flew regularly over North Vietnam, had pencilled a beard and mustache on the grave, pious, spotlighted face of the captured American.)

At the Chu Lai officers' club for Task Force Oregon, drinks were twenty cents each, and the pilots usually had three or four rounds each evening before supper. One pilot observed, "At these prices, you can't afford *not* to drink." On the evening of August 10th, the FAC pilots drove to the Marine dining hall, which was a favorite of theirs among the base's many dining halls. Ham, chops, steak, and chicken were served there. They were all prepared in the dependably appetizing style of an excellent truckers' diner on a big American highway, and you could have as much as you could eat. Some Korean officers sat grouped together at several tables. Most of them were enjoying the Korean version of r. and r.—a visit to an American base like Chu Lai, where they were allowed to eat in the American mess halls, shop in the American PX, and swim on the safe stretch of beach occupied by the base. Conversation at dinner usually revolved around matters having to do with the flying life. Often, the pilots discussed the day's events, sometimes criticizing or praising the accuracy of certain missions of fighter-bombers. They stuck fairly closely to day-to-day events and to the technical problems of bombing missions, such as what altitude is best to bomb from and how to tell if a bomb is "hung" on the wing after the bomb release has been triggered. This evening, they discussed an incident in which a pilot had spotted a man on the ground, had judged him to be a Vietcong soldier when he attempted to escape observation by running into a grove of trees, and had called in planes to bomb the trees. This incident, which in itself was quite ordinary, had one unusual aspect: the FAC pilot had been flying outside his assigned area, and the bombs had only just missed some American troops nearby.

Another pilot said that he, too, had spotted a Vietcong soldier and had later guided an air strike onto the woods the man had disappeared into.

I asked him how he had been able to tell that the man was a Vietcong soldier.

"Well, he walked real proud, with a kind of bounce in his gait, like a soldier, instead of just shuffling along, like the farmers do," the pilot answered.

During my stay with the FAC pilots, they never discussed the progress of the war as a whole, nor did they ever express any hatred for the enemy. They talked a lot about pensions and salaries, they complained about the administrative sloppiness of the promotion procedures, and they discussed the advantages of various cities for r.-and-r. tours (Thai women had good figures; Hong Kong had good cheap clothes, hi-fi equipment, and cameras). The pilots laughed when they read in the *News Sheet* that lectures on venereal diseases, and how to tell if you had any of them, were going to be given to the men just before they went on r.-and-r. tours. The armed services displayed a completely tolerant attitude toward the soldiers' patronage of brothels in Vietnam and in the Asian cities used for r.-and-r. tours. In Hong Kong, until very recently, the Army employed a prostitute of mixed Chinese and Portuguese parentage, who spoke understandable English, to brief the soldiers on how to pick up prostitutes among the city's bar girls without getting into fights or getting fleeced. The briefing was intended to minimize the ugly incidents that occur when a soldier is overcharged or misunderstands a girl's intentions. The pilots talked a great deal about the living conditions and the food on other bases. Once, at dinner, Captain Reese got into a long discussion about food with another pilot, and as he ate a plateful of ham, he gave a detailed description of a chicken dinner he had eaten at the Duc Pho base. Then, beginning on a piece of cake, he described to me the breakfast at the Marine dining hall in which he was eating at that moment. "They have terrific breakfasts here," he said. "Every day, they have eggs, bacon, pancakes with butter and maple syrup, toast, milk, raspberry jam, grapefruit juice, coffee, and tea—the works. Real fine breakfast."

Although the pilots never spoke angrily of the Vietcong, they often spoke disparagingly of the Army, compared to the Air Force; they called Army men "grunts." Their feeling about the Army seemed very much like one ball club's or college fraternity's feeling about a rival, but occasionally they expressed a bitterness that went beyond such friendly rivalry. One pilot told me, "The Army guys sometimes don't care what you have to do, so long as they get an air strike. But I'm not going to send men on an impossible mission to get killed like that. I'm responsible to the Air Force, too, and I've got to think of Air Force safety. Sometimes it's kind of hard, because you have to look a general in the eye and say, 'No, sir, I can't do that.'" I was surprised at the intensity of the rivalry not only between the services but between units in the same service. The men of the 1st Brigade of the 101st Airborne, who were extremely proud of their paratrooper training, referred contemptuously to all infantrymen as "legs."

Once, when I was driving inside the Chu Lai base on a cruelly hot afternoon with a paratrooper of the 101st, he refused to pick up a hitchhiking soldier, on the ground that the soldier was a "leg," and "no leg is worth picking up." High officers of the 101st and the 3rd of the 4th maligned each other, in my presence, by claiming that the other brigade's body count was falsified. "The 3rd of the 4th count the probables in their body count," an officer of the 101st told me. "We don't deal with probables. We only deal with confirmed kills counted by sight. That's the only way." On another occasion, an officer of the 3rd of the 4th made the same charge about the 101st, and added that the 101st's "weapons-kill ratio" was much worse than the 3rd of the 4th's, the implication being that the 101st was far less discriminating than the 3rd of the 4th when it came to deciding whom to kill. Men of both the Army and the Air Force made derogatory remarks about the Marines. One soldier of the 101st told me that the Marines were "no different from the Vietcong" in their handling of prisoners. I asked if he meant that they beat the prisoners. "Hell, *we* work 'em over before we talk to 'em," the soldier said. "The Marines are a lot worse than that. They're just like the V.C."

After dinner that evening, the pilots had a choice of two movies, one at an outdoor theatre on the beach near the Marine dining hall and the other up at the Task Force Oregon officers' club. The officers' club stood on the crest of a five-hundred-foot hill, overlooking a brushy meadow that swept down to the sea. A number of tables with chairs were arranged in a large, three-walled room under a broad, barnlike palm-leaf roof; the front was open to the ocean. In back, there was a long bar with a television set at one end, swivelling barstools, a dart board, and bartenders who wore gaudy Hawaiian shirts. Movies were shown in front.

The club commanded a view of the entire twenty-kilo-
metre crescent of beach. Even on the hottest, stillest day, a
fresh breeze blew in off the water. At night, out on the
ocean, the lamps that all local fishing boats were required
to keep burning after dark glowed from miles away. On
most evenings, the booming of artillery and bombing
sounded steadily, sometimes lighting up the night sky
down the coast. During some operations, flares, which are
fired by artillery or dropped from planes, and descend
slowly on parachutes, seemed to be hanging over the
mountains throughout the night. Two hundred yards from
the club, the helicopter landing pad for the base hospital
sat on a high ridge, from which there was a sharp drop to
the sea. Several times each day, a helicopter would fly up
the coast at full speed and settle rapidly onto the asphalt,
which was in full view of the front of the officers' club and
looked from there like a small black stage. Two figures
would run up to the helicopter and then run back to the
hospital, bearing a man on a stretcher. If the cloth over the
man covered him only up to his shoulders, the man was
wounded, but if the cloth covered his face the man had
died. Inside the club, the hospital landing pad was visible
only from a few front tables, and most of the officers did
not notice when a helicopter arrived, but when the officers
were standing in front of the club at their weekly outdoor
barbecue, tending their steaks in the charcoal pits, the
arrival of a helicopter at the hospital caused a brief
slackening in the din of conversation as the officers looked
up from their drinks and steaks to watch the two figures
bearing a wounded or dead man into the hospital.

Once every few weeks, on nights that did not precede
military operations or important pre-planned strikes, some
of the FAC pilots, I was told, would get together to get
drunk. One evening, Captain Reese and two other pilots,

whom I will call Major Nugent and Captain Leroy, returned to the FAC pilots' quarters from the officers' club
talking in booming voices and laughing loudly at everything any of them said. Major Nugent had apparently half-
seriously yielded to an Army officer's urging that he enter
airborne training school, and Captain Reese was snicker-
ing and teasing him about it. "Why would anyone want to
jump out of a perfectly good airplane? You must be out of
your gourd!" he exclaimed seven or eight times, provoking
a more uproarious laugh with each repetition. His idea
that you should stay in an airplane until it was shot down
reflected his loyalty to the Air Force and his contempt for
paratroopers. About midnight, when Captain Leroy was
on his way to bed, he tripped over someone's box of gear
and fell on the floor. Later that night, an unidentified
person threw a glass of water on another pilot as he slept.

On August 11th, the last
day of Operation Hood River, I flew on a FAC mission with
a pilot of about forty, whom I will call Major Billings.
Major Billings has slightly asymmetrical features, wide-
open, staring eyes, a somewhat hoarse voice, and a simple,
frank laugh from the belly which bursts forth suddenly on
one tone. He told me that he had flown in three wars and
had given up everything for the Air Force, including his
wife, who had divorced him because he was so rarely
stationed in the United States. He liked to tell the other
pilots, in his cheerful, straightforward manner, about his
problems with his girl friends back in the United States.
("They're all over fifty," he joked.) He told the other
pilots that he had been a Catholic until the Second World
War, but then had noticed that all the churchgoing pilots

seemed to be getting shot down, and had never gone to church since. He said that in civilian life he drove a sports car and always wore bright-red socks.

We took off in the early morning into a perfect blue sky. Major Billings had been assigned one pre-planned strike, and did not expect any immediate strikes to be called. Flying southwest from Chu Lai over the rubble and the abandoned fields that lay along the Song Tra Bong between Route 1 and the mountains, we soon reached the town of Tra Bong, which stood alone in the mountains, and then we turned south, crossed a ridge of mountains, and continued to a smaller ridge, which was indicated by the target coördinates. A few kilometres to the south of the target, in the valley of the Song Tra Khuc, Operation Hood River was coming to a close. To the north of the target, craters from a B-52 strike formed a line of yellow splashes on the flanks of many small, steep knobs and ridges in a high valley that looked from the air like a choppy sea. The top of the target ridge was covered for most of its length with fields cultivated by the Montagnards, but in one place, on top of a small cliff, there was a square patch of dense woods about two hundred yards on a side, and it was this that was the target. "A lot of Montagnard farming goes on up here," said Major Billings. "They grow rice and corn."

As we approached the wooded patch on the ridge, the Major pointed to a wisp of smoke that hung over the woods, and exclaimed, "Look at the smoke! See the smoke? That's Charlie having his breakfast!"

I asked him how he knew the smoke was from the fire of a Vietcong soldier.

"After a while, you get to know Charlie's habits," he said. "Now we'll leave the area, like we didn't know a thing. Even the Montagnards up here are under V.C.

control. We had troops in here a while ago, when Hood River began, but they've gone into the valley now. The Montagnards are a funny people. They live out in the open. Only the V.C. live under the trees. That whole hilltop is supposed to be a large base camp. I'll stay out of the area for an hour, until my flight comes in, so as not to arouse any undue activity on the V.C.'s part."

We turned north and began to circle over the town of Tra Bong. As we waited, a few snatches of conversation between ground units in the Song Tra Khuc Valley came over our radio. A voice said, "We were attacked by one Victor Charlie. He was an old guy, and he rushed our point man carrying a stick. The point man yelled at him to stop and then fired him up."

An answering voice laughed, and then said, "Sounds like a vicious attack," and laughed again.

The first voice said, "He seemed to be kind of doped up."

Major Billings remarked to me, "The V.C. often dope up their soldiers with marijuana before they go into a fight, so they won't be scared and will have good endurance. We've seen a lot of cases of that."

A minute later, a new voice on the ground said, "If you go much beyond that northernmost burning village, you'll be getting out of our area of operation."

"We picked up some weapons and a bunch of refugees," said another voice.

"We've captured two tons of rice," said yet another voice.

After we had circled for twenty minutes, three fighter-bombers reported their arrival in the area, and Major Billings immediately spotted them cutting across the sky above us. They reported that they were carrying, among them, six five-hundred-pound bombs and six canisters of napalm. Flying back to the target, Major Billings saw that the wisp of smoke was still hanging above the trees. "Oh, Daddy! This is the one I have been waiting for! They're *still* down here!" he exclaimed. Cutting back sharply, he bore down hard on the ridge, so that the woods filled the whole front windshield for five seconds or so, growing larger and larger. The rocket was fired off the wing with a loud explosion. Immediately, Major Billings pulled the craft's nose up sharply, thrusting both of us deep into our seats, and flew away from the ridge, leaving a puff of dense white smoke rising out of the trees about thirty yards south of the original wisp of smoke. "I want you to hit thirty yards above my smoke," he told the flight commander. Holding the plane in a continuous tight turn well below two nearby peaks, Major Billings watched the first fighter-bomber dive low over the patch of woods in a practice run. A second plane sent two bombs into the forest, and they struck about a hundred yards from the original wisp of smoke. "Oh, nice! Nice!" exclaimed Major Billings.

He told the flight commander, "Try to get those next ones up a little higher, right above my smoke there."

The next bomb load missed the forest completely and landed in a field of brush.

"I want you to get it right near my smoke," the Major repeated.

"Yeah, sorry," the flight commander answered.

The next plane sent its bombs onto the top of the ridge, within thirty yards of the first wisp of smoke.

"Nice, baby—beautiful. A good shot there," said the Major.

A plane sent two canisters of napalm onto the opposite side of the ridge, into some woods at the bottom of the cliffs.

"That's the wrong side there," said the Major.

A second load of napalm splashed into the forest about fifty yards west of the smoke from Major Billings' rocket, and a third, and final, load splashed about thirty yards south of his smoke.

We flew in and circled three or four hundred feet above the woods, banking so sharply that the ground seemed to be directly below the left side of the plane. Clouds of dust from the bombs and black smoke from the napalm rose from the woods. Unspent napalm was burning itself out in a few small patches, and the five-hundred-pound bombs had made gaps about eight feet across in the trees. A pungent odor of dust, seared leaves, and smoke reached us as we flew over the destroyed woods. After a moment or two, Major Billings pulled out of the dizzying corkscrew turn and, addressing the flight commander, said, "Where that smoke was coming from—there's nothing there. You got it real well. A real nice job. I'll give you eighty per cent of Bombs on Target, because of those two shots down the hill. Thanks very much. We'll see you another day."

To me, Major Billings added, "I don't know what kind of people were down there, but they're not there now."

Since it would be an hour before the next FAC plane came to relieve him, Major Billings decided to fly east to the entrance of the Song Tra Khuc Valley, where the 1st Brigade of the 101st Airborne was concluding Operation Hood River. "You can't see anything from fifteen hundred feet," the Major said, and as we passed out of the mountains and over the populated coastal plain, he swooped down to about a hundred and fifty feet and began to fly in a continuous S pattern, to make it difficult for snipers on the ground to take aim at the plane. Men of the 101st were burning the houses on the plain just north of the Song Tra Khuc. From a few hundred yards away and an altitude of under a hundred feet, the orange flames of the houses and the green moving figures of the men wavered wildly in heat waves billowing off the plain, and sometimes were almost blotted out by them. Major Billings continued his twisting, low-altitude explorations, and we suddenly came in view of a figure dressed in black, walking along a path that divided two fields and led into a shady grove where a house was still standing. The Major cut the plane sharply left and rushed low over the person on the path, who stopped walking and looked up. "Ah, it's just an old lady," he said to me. "She isn't *supposed* to be here. They were given twenty-four hours to get out, but they keep wandering back in. That's one of the big problems. You tell them they're not supposed to come into the free-strike zone or they'll get shot, and they keep coming back in. If they're men, they're just one of two things—draft dodgers or V.C."

I asked what the official policy toward people who left the camps and returned to their homes was.

"You can't always be sure what they are, but if a place is thoroughly infested with V.C. the province chief gives us permission to destroy the place," he said.

At that moment, we flew over a stream running through the fields, and Major Billings spotted three boys sitting naked in a little pool, taking a bath and looking up at our plane. "Look!" said Major Billings. "They're hiding down there! But this is out of our area of operation."

We had flown several miles north of the valley entrance. Here and there among the ruins, groups of houses remained standing. People walked along the paths near these, and children played in several of the courtyards, but few fields had been left unmarked by artillery and bomb craters.

I asked the Major how he distinguished members of the Vietcong from the rest of the population.

"If they run is one way," he said. "There are a lot of

ways. Sometimes, when you see a field of people, it looks like just a bunch of farmers. Now, you see, the Vietnamese people—they're not interested in the U.S. Air Force, and they don't look at the planes going over them. But down in that field you'll see *one guy* whose conical hat keeps bobbing up and down. He's looking, because he wants to know where you're going. So you make a couple of passes over the field, and then one of them makes a break for it—it's the guy that was lookin' up at you—and he's your V.C. So you look where he goes, and call in an air strike. You can split up the V.C.s and the innocent civilians that way. There are a hundred ways of telling a V.C. It gets to be second nature. Sometimes you see the V.C.s hiding by plastering themselves against the wall of one of those paddies. One trouble is, aside from these rockets, we don't have any weapons. But once I about ran a guy to death. I caught him out in the open, and I'd make a pass and he'd run for it, and then I'd make a pass in the other direction and he'd run the opposite way. Then he'd hide in some trees, and when I'd make a pass at him he'd make a break for it. I must have chased him for about an hour before I got some planes to put in a strike."

I said that this seemed to amount to a technique of sniping with bombs.

"That's it. You could say that," he answered.

Later, back at the FAC pilots' quarters, Major Billings told me, "I guess you can call it a kind of intuition. I think I can just about *smell* a V.C. from five thousand feet by now. Like everything else, some people have got the knack and some people don't. Some people wouldn't be able to tell a V.C. no matter *how* long they tried."

That evening, Operation Hood River came to a close, and the troops rested in the field for a day and received fresh supplies as they prepared for the new operation.

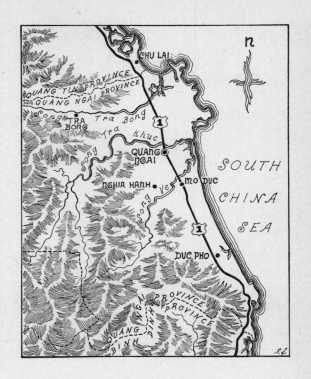

On August 13, 1967, two days after Operation Hood River came to an end, Task Force Oregon launched Operation Benton. In Quang Ngai Province I had seen the results of the American bombing, shelling, and ground activity but, for the most part, I had not seen the destruction take place. Now I was about to observe in detail the process of destruction as it unfolded in Operation Benton, in which Task Force Oregon went over the northern border of Quang Ngai into Quang Tin Province. I spent several days flying in FAC planes attached to the 1st Brigade of the 101st Airborne. On August 12th, I flew over the area where Operation Benton was to be carried out. This was a three-hour reconnaissance mission, with a pilot whom I will call Major Ingersol. Major Ingersol was a few years older than the other pilots, and he was more reserved. At the FAC pilots' quarters on the base at Chu Lai, he often read paperback mysteries or other novels while the rest of the pilots joked together. When he did enter into the conversation, he ordinarily spoke in serious, measured tones, which did not quite fit in with the usual light banter. Once, when the other pilots were sitting around drinking and discussing the figures of Thai bar girls, his contribution to the conversation was "I've heard that there are some exquisite restaurants in Bangkok." Another time, while chatting with a captain in the FAC central control room, he expressed a keen appreciation of the natural beauty of Quang Ngai. "It's a lovely countryside," he said. "One of my favorite activities is following waterfalls up through the valleys. It's a shame we have to destroy it."

While Major Ingersol and I were flying to the area of the new operation, he described to me his method of distinguishing Vietcong soldiers from the rest of the population. "You know that they are V.C.s if they shoot at you or if you see them carrying a weapon. Those are about the only two ways," he said. In the matter of trails through the woods, he had subtler criteria. As we passed over the flank of a tall mountain, he pointed out a trail, almost as wide as a small road, that ran up the mountainside from the valley. The trees were tall and dense, and the path was visible as an occasional gap in the jungle foliage. About halfway up the mountain, this large, clearly distinguishable trail began to get narrower. For a stretch, it apparently continued under the dense foliage, because farther up the mountain it became visible once again, but then it was lost to sight altogether, "This is the kind of thing we look for," Major Ingersol said. "See how that trail disappears up there? That indicates to us that there is probably a base camp up there. These trails that go up into the mountains and disappear are often V.C. trails. Also, we look to see if the trails have been freshly used."

I remarked that from fifteen hundred feet it must be very difficult to tell whether a trail that was mostly covered by dense jungle foliage had been used recently.

"Even then you can tell," Major Ingersol said. "You see, the V.C. use water buffalo and other large animals to carry their equipment around, and they leave marks. These trails often get hit by artillery fire at night." As we flew over a thirty-foot-wide crater that had eliminated one section of a footpath, Major Ingersol commented, "Now look down there. See how someone has built the trail

around the crater? This is the kind of sign you look for."
He said that he also looked for bunkers to recommend as
bombing targets. And, as still another example of the kind
of suspicious sign he looked for on his reconnaissance
missions, he told me that in one small field high in the
mountains there was a small herd of water buffalo that
disappeared from sight every few days. "We speculate that
the V.C. use those water buffalo to carry things," he said.

Major Ingersol spent most of his three hours flying over
a maze of little hills and valleys, for these were to be the
scene of Operation Benton. The area of operation was a
rectangle of about ten by twenty kilometres lying southwest of Phuoc Tien, a town in the southern part of Quang
Tin Province. The 1st Brigade of the 101st was to launch
the operation the next morning in an area ten kilometres
on a side, and two days later some units of the 196th were
to be lifted into an area of equal size to the east. I had
decided that, within the area of operation, I would concentrate my attention on a somewhat smaller area, clearly
discernible both on aviation maps and on the ground, and
observe it from FAC planes on as many of the first few days
of Operation Benton as I could, in order to see how
bombings were carried out during a large military operation. Just southwest of Phuoc Tien, which lies in a valley
of rice fields surrounded by foothills, two small rivers—the
Song Tien and the Song Tram—join to form a single
stream, called the Song Chang. (The Vietnamese word
"song" means "river.") Within the fork of the rivers
stands a small mountain, about a thousand feet high, called
Chop Vum and around its base there were at that time a
number of villages and scattered houses. To the south of
Chop Vum, a narrow dirt road ran east and west through
thickly settled fields. I decided to observe an area six

kilometres square surrounding Chop Vum, and henceforth I will refer to this as the Chop Vum area. It was bordered, roughly, on the east by the Song Tien, on the west by the Song Tram, on the south by the road, and on the north by the Song Tien again, for this river bends sharply to the west after flowing north for about six kilometres. Between Chop Vum and these boundaries, just beyond which rose an encircling range of two- to three-thousand-foot mountains, spread a landscape of tiny forested hills, seldom more than fifty feet high, standing like chains of islands in a sea of small terraced rice fields. A few of the knolls and knobs were smooth-topped and rolling, but most of them were very steep, and rose abruptly from the rice fields, like miniature models of the mountains surrounding them. Most of the houses were not in villages but stood scattered among the fields. Wherever the land was only gently inclined, it had been terraced and planted with crops. Along the sharp ridge of one small hill, a footpath ran to a small pocket of flat land near the top. In this pocket, farmers had planted rice and built several houses that commanded a view of most of the valley and the mountains beyond. Nearly all the houses near Chop Vum had front yards where chickens and ducks could run about, vegetable gardens in back, and a ring of hedges and trees around house, yard, and garden. One species of palm tree, which had a single crown of leaves and grew to be fifty or sixty feet high, was particularly common in the gardens. Small, winding paths ran from house to house on top of the field divides and up and around the knobby hills, and every crevice or fold in the skirts of the mountains seemed to have a house tucked in it. The arrangement of the houses allowed a dense population to live separate lives with considerable privacy. In only a few places were as many as fifty or sixty houses grouped together to form villages, and even in these places the houses were not lined up side by side on streets but were separated by yards and by groves of bamboos and palms. The layout of the villages conformed to the bumps and hollows of the landscape, instead of dominating it with a symmetrical design. The village houses were linked by paths, and these paths led, ultimately, into an indistinct, curving main path that ran near all the houses. The village of Phai Tay stood at the base of Chop Vum, within the fork of the Song Tram and the Song Tien; the village of Duc Tan stood on the north bank of the Song Tien about two kilometres northeast of Phai Tay; and the village of Thanh Phuoc was sprawled along both sides of the road that formed the southern boundary of the area. In Thanh Phuoc, two stone churches stood within fifty yards of each other on opposite sides of the road. Each of them was about three stories high and seventy feet long, was faced with intricately carved stucco, and had a cross on the roof.

The afternoon I flew over this landscape with Major Ingersol, several herds of water buffalo were wallowing in the clear water of the rivers. There were people bent over at work in the water of the rice fields, and in the yards. The area had been heavily battered at some earlier date, and gray and red squares of what had once been houses dotted the landscape. Roughly one house in twenty had been destroyed. Many fields were totally taken up by craters, and the forest on the hillsides was blackened and pockmarked. On two adjacent knolls, perhaps a hundred feet high and five hundred feet wide at their bases, the woods had been almost entirely destroyed by bombs that had left overlapping craters. Each type of terrain—the mountains, the fields, and the yards of the houses—seemed to have received the same amount of bombing, as though the fighter-bomber pilots' intent had been to cover with equal quantities of explosives the areas marked out by the squares on their maps. Smaller craters, from artillery fire, spotted the fields and yards but were not large enough to show up in the thick forest. Many of the artillery craters were yellow and fresh, but all the bomb craters were partly overgrown with bushes and vines, and so must have been at least several months old.

I asked Major Ingersol when these bombings had occurred, and he answered, "Well, only the Marines were operating around here before Task Force Oregon arrived, but I don't think they got up this far. But it looks like they did. I don't know. It looks like it happened quite a long time ago, anyway."

Having surveyed the future area of operation, Major Ingersol flew south across several ridges of mountains toward the Song Tra Khuc Valley, in northern Quang Ngai Province. On the way, he indulged in his favorite pastime of viewing waterfalls. "You can see that FAC-ing *can* be pretty boring, especially on these strictly V.R. missions," he said. "V.R." stands for "visual reconnaissance." "I'll show you some of the waterfalls up here. They're just beautiful. This is some of the most beautiful mountain countryside I have ever seen." Before we came to a waterfall, he would describe it to me in detail from memory, telling me whether or not it had a pool at the bottom, whether it cascaded over a cliff or flowed down the rocks, and how many tiers it had. One of his favorite waterfalls—a long, cascading one with a large, clear pool in a rock bed at the base—had been bombed since he last saw it; he pointed out a crater on its lip.

By the time we started back to Chu Lai, it was late afternoon, and the sun was large and red beyond the dark mountain ridges. Over the plane's radio, a voice from somewhere said, "Hey, we're having a party over in D 19 tonight, with lots of free booze. Come on over."

Another voice answered, "I'll make it if I can, but I don't know if I'll be able to get over tonight. Thanks a lot."

Early the next morning, Operation Benton was launched in the area I had just flown over with Major Ingersol. The men of the 1st Brigade of the 101st Airborne Division were beginning their fifth consecutive week in the field. On the evening of the twelfth, the FAC pilots for the 1st of the 101st had only one drink each before dinner and did not drink at all after dinner. During a final planning session at quarters that evening, the lower officers called their superiors "sir" regularly, for the first time in the two days I had spent with them. Their mission for the next day was to guide air strikes onto the four initial landing zones, or L.Z.s, for helicopters bearing the troops into the area. These air strikes were a general practice, and were termed "L.Z. preps." Just before the troops were landed, the landing zones were "hosed down" with machine-gun and rocket fire from helicopters.

During the first two days of the operation, the back seat of every FAC plane that went up was occupied by an artillery observer, so I was unable to fly, but in the evenings the FAC pilots told me something of what they had seen. They said that, at the last minute before the L.Z. preps were to start, one flight of planes had been cancelled, owing to mechanical failure, so one landing zone had received only the machine-gun and rocket fire from helicopters. At a second landing zone, the L.Z. prep had been applied to a plot of high fields, according to plan, but the troops had mistakenly landed a kilometre away, on a hilltop that had not been blown up for them in advance. Meanwhile, seven or eight kilometres away, at an artillery battery that was to give support to the L.Z. preps and to the operation itself as it got under way, a helicopter had crashed into an ammunition truck, setting off the ammunition and blowing up the battery and inflicting several casualties, so no further artillery support could be given to any of the landing zones from that position. The installation of the command post for the operation, on top of a small mountain just north of the Song Tien at the point where it starts to bend north, had gone smoothly at first, but then a fire had broken out on the landing zone. (According to the FAC pilots, the air strikes they directed never started fires. It was the helicopters, they maintained, that started the fires, with their machine guns and their rockets.) When more than a hundred men, several artillery pieces, and several crates of ammunition had been landed, the fire had got out of control. Artillery shells had begun to explode in the flames, and the troops had evacuated the spot and set up a camp on a nearby hilltop, temporarily leaving several damaged artillery pieces and mortars behind. The men and equipment of the command post itself had been removed by helicopter to the top of a mountain about five kilometres to the east. Artillery shells had continued to explode sporadically on the flaming hilltop of the old command post for several hours. Over the next two days, seven more landings were completed without serious accident.

The first afternoon, the troops received occasional

sniper fire as they dug their positions into the hills. The ground commander on the hill next to the abandoned command post judged that the snipers were N.V.A. troops firing from the village of Duc Tan, which was about a kilometre west of the hilltop, and he requested that the village be bombed. A grave, wooden-faced young FAC pilot, whom I will call Lieutenant Moore, guided the air strikes, and later reported that twenty or thirty houses had been destroyed. In telling his fellow-pilots about the air strikes, he said, "I flattened the whole place, but I just couldn't get this *one* hootch." "Hootch" is the Army term for a Vietnamese house. "I kept telling them to put it right on this one hootch, and there must be six thousand-pound-bomb craters right around there, but I just couldn't get it," he went on. "Now it's a matter of *principle* with me to get that hootch. You watch—I'm going to get it." That day, several other bombings took place, in scattered parts of the area of operation. When night fell, an enemy force of undetermined size attacked the troops that had moved from the original command post to the adjacent hill. Some of the enemy went up on the evacuated hill and fired the mortar shells that the men of the 1st of the 101st had left there when they moved to their new position, and at the same time enemy soldiers attacked the new position. Ground commanders requested artillery strikes, and they also called in the principal weapon for air support at night—the AC-47 (this was the military version of the DC-3, and was nicknamed Spooky) armed with three 7.62-mm. machine guns, called miniguns, which could fire a hundred rounds per second. The AC-47 dropped flares, which, as they parachuted down, illuminated the ground below them as brightly as daylight, yet not even rough accuracy was possible in these conditions, and the technique was to spray with minigun fire the entire area in which the enemy was presumed to be operating. On the first night of the operation, one Spooky expended all its ammunition, which amounted to 21,300 rounds. It was later reported that four Americans and thirty-five of the enemy had been killed in the fight. During the preceding day, a helicopter had been downed by enemy fire. (Throughout the rest of the operation, which lasted about two weeks, an average of one helicopter a day was downed by enemy fire. Some of the wreckage was airlifted out of the area by large Chinook helicopters, and other wreckage was demolished on the ground by rockets from helicopters still aloft, to prevent the enemy from getting the guns, radios, and other equipment. In at least one case, the enemy entered a downed helicopter and took some of the equipment before the helicopter could be destroyed. The downing of the dozen or so helicopters during the operation was not mentioned in the press releases of the final week, and the Army would not confirm a total figure, but it extended every hospitality to any reporter who wished to see the operation himself, from the air or on the ground, or to talk with the men who had taken part in it. While I was aloft over the area of operation, I often saw Chinook helicopters heading back over the mountains toward the base with the wrecks of the smaller Huey helicopters hanging from their bellies by cables.)

A press release from the Information Office of the 1st Brigade of the 101st Airborne Division, titled "Paratroopers Maul NVA Battalion," described the encounter with the enemy:

> NUI CHUONG, Vietnam (101-IO) —Fires from exploding artillery shells blossomed around the hill. Flames leaped high in the dry elephant grass sending a black plume of smoke into the cloudless sky.

Captain Ronald G. Odom, San Francisco, looked out the helicopter door at the burning hilltop. . . .

After recounting several light contacts with the enemy during the day, the release continued:

Moonlight played across the hilltop casting grotesque shadows that kept the eyes of every paratrooper strained, nerves taut.

The moon disappeared at 11:30 P.M. Minutes later the enemy attacked!

"They opened up with everything they had," Odom recounted. "We were hit with 81- and 60-mm. mortar fire. Off our flank, their heavy machine guns began firing and their infantry moved in."

Odom previously had made a map reconnaissance of likely locations for enemy mortars and Nemetz called in artillery. Despite the artillery support, the enemy continued to rake B Co. with mortars and automatic weapons.

On the northwest flank, a Bostonian, Lt. Robert Berry, and his 4th platoon were taking the brunt of the attack. He radioed: "Some are ten meters away. Good hand grenade range. Out."

Odom recalled how he responded to Berry's report: "He was so damn cool, I couldn't believe it, and he stayed cool and calm all night long."

Lt. Thomas J. Courtney, Knoxville, Tenn., had the 3rd platoon firing into the enemy pushing toward his flank. The tracers from their rifles criss-crossed their perimeter with streaks of red.

The enemy mortar fire continued to blast

away on the hill. Suddenly, a report from Berry's platoon announced the location of the Communist mortars—barely 100 meters from his platoon.

Forward observer Nemetz pinpointed the location and called in a thundering volume of fire. . . .

Throughout the night, Col. Puckett encouraged his men. He braved mortar fire to aid the wounded, walked the perimeter to talk with the troops.

At 2 A.M., nearly nine hours after the battle started, it stopped.

Silence surrounded the paratroopers as they waited for dawn.

When day came, the tired men of B Co. surveyed their perimeter. Thirty-five NVA lay dead, their weapons scattered over the battlefield.

On the second day, the 1st of the 101st began to spread out into the countryside in small units; several of them met heavy resistance from the enemy and suffered casualties. That night, the FAC pilots said that the unit ground commanders had called for an unusually large number of air strikes throughout the area of operation. The pilots described the targets to each other in terms of topographical features, or by coördinates on their maps, because they did not know the names of any of the towns or rivers in the area. One FAC pilot remarked that the units involved in Operation Benton must be "really kill-hungry," for three of the companies had chosen as code designations for themselves the names Cutthroat, Marauder, and Assassin.

On the morning of the third day of Operation Benton, I

flew over the 1st of the 101st's area of operation with Major Billings, whom I had flown with during Operation Hood River. I saw that, except for two or three houses, the village of Duc Tan, which had stood below the evacuated command post, had been destroyed. Some groups of houses in Duc Tan had been completely annihilated by bombs; the only traces of their former existence were their wells or back gardens. Other houses had been burned to the ground by napalm. Most of the fields around the destroyed village had been eliminated by the deep craters of delayed-fuse bombs or else had been covered with debris. More craters were scattered across other fields in the Chop Vum area and across mountainsides, and the gray squares of freshly burned individual houses dotted most of the landscape. Major Billings told me that these houses had been burned by phosphorus rockets fired from helicopter "gunship" patrols. A few minutes later, I watched a gunship cruise low over the landscape. It wheeled suddenly and fired several phosphorus rockets into a group of three houses that stood in a clump of palms. White smoke puffed up, and the houses burst into flames. The helicopter circled and then charged the houses again, firing more rockets into the fields and gardens. Several hilltops and small mountains that had been green and wooded when I saw them three days earlier were burned black by napalm. Fresh artillery craters were spattered over the fields around the landing zones. At that point, approximately twenty per cent of the houses in the Chop Vum area had been destroyed.

Major Billings had been assigned to guide a "preplanned strike," but before he could locate the target on the ground a ground commander called for an "immediate" strike, which meant a strike carried out a few hours, at most, after it was requested, whether by a ground commander or by a FAC pilot. "We picked up some sniper fire earlier this morning from a couple of hootches down below us, at about 384 297, and we'd like you to hit it for us," the ground commander said. Major Billings flew over the hundred-metre square described by the coördinates, and found that it included the two large stone churches along the road, in the village of Thanh Phuoc. The ground commander was in charge of a hilltop landing zone that was a little over half a kilometre from the churches. When he had received the sniper fire, he had apparently scanned the horizon, noticed the two church steeples, which were the only buildings that stuck up above the lines of trees, and decided that the snipers were firing from the churches. In front of one church, a white flag flew from the top of a pole as high as the church itself.

"Let's have a look and see what's down there," said Major Billings. He took our plane on a low pass over the churches. The churches were surrounded by twenty or thirty houses. About half of these had stone walls and red tile roofs. The others had clay-and-bamboo walls and thatched roofs. One thatch-roofed building was perhaps fifty feet long and thirty feet wide, and appeared to be some sort of gathering place. Flower gardens were in bloom in front of both churches. Behind both, plots of vegetables stretched back through glades of palm trees to rice fields. After climbing to fifteen hundred feet again, Major Billings got into contact with the ground commander and said, "Two of those structures seem to be structures of worship. Do you want them taken out?"

"Roger," the ground commander replied.

"There seems to be a white flag out front there," Major Billings said.

"Yeah. Beats me what it means," the ground commander replied.

An hour later, three F-4 fighter-bombers reached the target area, and the flight commander radioed to Major Billings—who had spent the time trying to spot suspicious activities—to say that they were prepared to strike with seven-hundred-and-fifty-pound bombs, rockets, and 20 mm.-cannon strafing fire.

"We can use all that good stuff," said Major Billings.

"What kind of a target is it?" asked the flight commander.

"They're military structures. You can tell by how they look that they're military structures," Major Billings answered. Just then a fleet of ten helicopters moving in tight formation arrived at the hilltop landing zone. Major Billings went on to say that he would have to wait until the helicopters left before he gave clearance to bomb.

I asked him whether he thought it was necessary to bomb the churches.

"Well, if the V.C. don't care and just go in there and use the place to fire on our troops, then we've got to wipe it out," Major Billings said. "And the V.C.—the V.C. are *the first ones to blow up a church*. They go after the churches on purpose, because the churches won't always go along with what the V.C. are doing. *They* don't care at all about blowing up a church and killing innocent civilians."

As the helicopters rose from the hilltop, Major Billings said to the flight commander, "Believe it or not, two of those big buildings down there are churches. I'll check with the ground commander again to see if he wants them taken out."

"No kidding!" said the flight commander.

"Say, do you want those two churches hit down there?" Major Billings asked the ground commander.

"That's affirmative," the ground commander replied.

"O.K., here goes," said the Major. Then, addressing the F-4 pilots, he said, "Make your passes from south to north. I'll circle over here to the west."

The Major brought the O-1 into a dive, aiming its nose at the village, and fired a phosphorus rocket. Its white smoke rose from a patch of trees fifty yards to the south of one church. "Do you see my smoke?" he asked the flight commander.

"Yeah, I got you," the flight commander said. "I'll make a dry run and then come in with the seven-hundred-and-fifty-pounders."

A minute later, an F-4 appeared from the south, diving low over the churches in a practice run. As it pulled out of its dive, it cut eastward and began to circle back for the next pass. A second F-4 made its dive in the same way, and released its bombs. A tall cloud of brown smoke rolled up from the vegetable garden in back of one of the churches.

"That's about a hundred metres off," Major Billings said. "See if you can move it forward."

"O.K. Sorry," the flight commander said.

The third plane also sent its bombs into the vegetable garden. The first plane, on its second pass, sent its bombs into rice fields about sixty yards to one side of the churches. Three pillars of brown smoke now rose several hundred feet in the air, dwarfing the churches and the houses. On the second plane's second pass, a bomb hit the back of one church directly—the church with the white flag on the pole in front.

"Oh, that's nice, baby, real nice," Major Billings said. "You're layin' those goodies right in there!"

When the smoke cleared, the church was gone except for its façade, which stood by itself, with its cross on top. The white flag still flew from its pole. The third plane sent its bombs into the rice fields to the side. The first plane fired rockets on its third pass, and they landed in the vegetable garden behind the destroyed church, leaving it smoking with dozens of small brown puffs. Several of the rockets from the next volley hit the other church, obliterating its back half and leaving two holes the size of doors in the roof of the front half. Four or five of the houses around the church burst into flame.

"That's real fine!" said Major Billings.

"Where do you want the twenty mike-mike?" asked the flight commander. ("Twenty mike-mike" is military slang for 20-mm.-cannon strafing fire, which fires a hundred explosive shells per second.)

"Lay it right down that line you've been hitting," Major Billings said. "Put it right down across those hootches, and we'll see if we can start a few fires." (Strafing rounds often set houses on fire, whereas bombs rarely do.)

As one of the F-4s made the first strafing run, the path of fire cut directly through the group of houses around the churches, sparkling for a fraction of a second with hundreds of brilliant flashes.

"Goody, goody! That's right down the line!" exclaimed Major Billings. "Why don't you just get those hootches by the other church, across the road, now?"

"Roger," answered the flight commander.

On the second strafing pass, the flashing path of shells cut across the group of houses on the other side of the road.

"Real fine!" Major Billings said. "Now how about getting that hootch down the road a bit?" He was referring to a tile-roofed house that stood in a field about a hundred yards to the west of one church. The path of fire from the third strafing pass—the final pass of the strike—cut directly across the house, opening several large holes in its roof.

"Right down the line!" Major Billings said. "Thanks, boys. You did a real fine job. I'm going to give you ninety-per-cent Target Coverage."

"Did I get any K.B.A.s?" the flight commander asked. (The number of killings credited to each pilot is not kept as an official statistic, but most pilots try to keep track of their K.B.A.s informally.)

Major Billings, who told me he had not seen any people in the area, either before or during the strike, answered, "I don't know—you'll have to wait until ground troops go in there sometime. But I'd say there were about four."

As the two men were talking, perhaps a dozen houses in the strafed area began to burn. First, the flames ate holes in the roofs, and then they quickly spread to the walls, turning each house into a ball of flame. Most of the houses burned to the ground within a few minutes, leaving columns of black smoke rising from the ruins.

Major Billings called Chu Lai to give his Bomb Damage Assessment Report. "There were two Permanent Military Structures Destroyed, ten Military Structures Destroyed, and five Damaged," he said.

I asked him whether he considered the houses and the churches military structures.

"Oh, that's just what we call them," he replied.

A few minutes later, the ground commander on the hilltop got in touch with Major Billings to request another immediate strike. "There's a row of bunkers down below our hill here, along a tree line, and we've seen the V.C.s down there," the ground commander said. "We see their heads poppin' in and out. We'd like to get an air strike put in down there."

Major Billings flew over the spot the ground commander had indicated, and found a line of trees about half a kilometre from the hill. The dark openings of several bunkers showed on the near side, and a row of several houses was standing on the far side.

"I've got you," Major Billings said. "Do you want us to put 'em in along that tree line down there? There are a couple of hootches down there, too."

"Affirmative. We've been getting trouble from that whole general area down there."

"O.K.," said Major Billings wearily, pronouncing the first syllable long and high, and the second low. "We'll do that as soon as the fighters come in."

Three F-4s arrived in the area twenty minutes later, and the flight commander announced that they were carrying napalm and thousand-pound bombs, which are the largest normally used in South Vietnam.

The first bombs of the strike landed about a hundred metres off target. One bomb turned an entire rice field into a crater about thirty-five feet across and six feet deep, and splashed mud over the surrounding fields. The next two bombs annihilated two houses with direct hits. Two more bombs landed next to the tree line, breaking most of the trees in half and hurling one palm tree fifty or sixty metres into a field.

"O.K., you got that tree line real good," Major Billings said. "Now let's get some of those hootches to the south of it with the napes." He directed the pilots to a group of a dozen houses that stood about forty yards from the tree line. The first canister landed beside two houses, which were instantly engulfed in napalm. When the smoke cleared, only the broken, blackened frames of the houses remained in the intense blaze, which continued after the houses were burned to the ground, because the napalm itself had not yet finished burning.

"Beautiful!" cried Major Billings. "You guys are right on target today!"

The next canister did not land directly on any of the houses, but it landed close enough to splash napalm over four of them, and these houses immediately burned down.

With the strike completed, Major Billings told the fighter-bomber pilots, "I'm giving you a hundred-per-cent Target Coverage. Thank you very much. It's been a pleasure to work with you. See you another day."

"Thank *you*," the flight commander answered.

Major Billings' three hours of flying time were up, and he turned the plane toward Chu Lai. Fifteen minutes later, we landed.

After we had taxied to a halt at the fuel pump, a young mechanic asked, "How'd it go, Major? Did you get some of 'em today?" He spoke with a nonchalance that failed to disguise his intense interest in getting an answer.

Instead of just replying "I dunno," or "Real fine," as he and the other pilots usually did, Major Billings burst out "We bombed two churches!" and gave a laugh that seemed to register his own surprise and wonderment at the act.

That afternoon, back at the FAC pilots' quarters, Major Billings, scratching his head and staring into the faces of the other pilots, exclaimed, again with a laugh, "I put in a strike on two churches!"

"No kidding," said one.

"They had a white flag in front of them. That damn white flag is still standing," the Major said.

"Yeah, I saw the white flag when I was out today," Lieutenant Moore said. "We'll have to get that white flag. It's a matter of *principle*."

The conversation turned to the subject of accidental bombings, and Major Billings, who had been a bomber pilot in both the Second World War and the Korean War, told of an ill-conceived bombing run he had once made over North Korea. "There was a big building right in the center of a town, and they told me it was a real important military headquarters," he said. "The target was so important that they sent two reconnaissance planes to guide me right to it. I laid my stuff all over it. About three days later, I found out that the place was really a school, and about a hundred children had been killed. They weren't going to tell me about the mistake, but I found out."

A man I have called Major Nugent said, "In early '65, there was a pilot who accidentally bombed an orphanage and killed a lot of kids. When he found out about it, he was so shook up that he voluntarily grounded himself for good. He said that he'd never fly again."

"That's the way you feel when something like that happens," said a man I have called Captain Reese, whom I'd also flown with during Operation Hood River.

"No—I mean, you can't let it get to you, or you couldn't go on," Major Billings objected. "It gets completely impersonal. After you've done it for a while, you forget that there are people down there."

"Yeah, everything looks so calm up where we are," Major Nugent said. "We can't even tell when we're getting shot at. We forget what's going on down on the ground. It's the guys on the ground—the ground troops—that really have it rough. They really know what's happening."

The extreme solemnity that had descended on the group seemed suddenly to generate an opposite impulse of hilarity, and small, irrepressible smiles began to appear on the pilots' faces.

Captain Reese turned to me and asked if I had ever

heard the songs about the war that they occasionally sang.

I said that I had heard one such song.

"Shall we tell him?" he asked the other pilots. They all looked at each other, and before anyone could answer, Captain Reese sang rapidly:

> "Strafe the town and kill the people,
> Drop napalm in the square,
> Get out early every Sunday
> And catch them at their morning prayer."

Major Billings then recited the words of another song:

> "Throw candy to the ARVN,
> Gather them all around,
> Take your twenty mike-mike
> And mow the bastards down."

At dinner in the Marine dining hall that evening, after a few drinks, the pilots began to make jokes in which they ridiculed the idea that the bombings they guided were unnecessarily brutal by inventing remarks that might be made by men so bloodthirsty that they took delight in intentionally killing innocents. The joke-tellers appeared to bring out their remarks with considerable uneasiness and embarrassment, and some of the pilots appeared to laugh unduly long in response, as though to reassure the tellers. All the jokes seemed to deal, indirectly, with the conflicts of conscience that had arisen in the conversation at the pilots' quarters during the afternoon.

When the main course was nearly finished, Major Nugent asked Captain Reese, "Git any woman and children today?"

"Yeah, but I let a pregnant woman get away," Captain Reese answered.

Lieutenant Moore's heavy-browed, serious, wooden face began to reflect a struggle between his usual gravity and a rebellious smile. "When we kill a pregnant woman, we count it as two V.C.—one soldier and one cadet," he said.

Everyone laughed loudly.

"Bruce got a bunch of kids playing marbles," said Major Nugent.

The group laughed again.

"I got an old lady in a wheelchair," Lieutenant Moore said, and there was more laughter.

"You know, when I flew over Japan, *anything* was fair game," Major Billings said. "They really were merciless, and they shot at everything. I remember I once saw an old guy riding a bicycle down the road, and I came up behind him, putting my fire in the road. The guy's feet started going faster and faster on the pedals, and just before my fire caught up with him you would never believe how fast the old bugger's feet were flying!"

The idea that civilians were often killed in the bombings they guided rarely arose in the pilots' conversation, and now that it had come up—if only to be debunked—the pilots made their jokes in the casual, familiar tone that marked most of their conversations. Yet the laugh that followed Major Billings' story erupted with a sudden force that seemed to take the men themselves by surprise. I sensed that their laughter eased a tension that had been building up during the session of jokes—eased it, perhaps, because this usually straightforward, informal group of men had found it a strain to have a largely undiscussed subject standing between them. Lieutenant Moore was so severely racked with laughter that he could not swallow a mouthful of food, and for several seconds he was convulsed silently and had to bend his head low with his hands over his mouth. Tears came to his eyes and to Major Nugent's.

"Oh, my!" Lieutenant Moore sighed, exhausted by all the laughing. Then he said, "I didn't kill that woman in the wheelchair, but she sure bled good!"

Nobody laughed at this joke. A silence ensued. Finally, Captain Reese suggested that they find out what movies were playing on the base that night.

The next afternoon, I flew on a FAC mission with Captain Leroy, a tall young pilot with a cocky, boyish smile, who was almost always relaxed and cheerful but, when the situation called for it, could pull himself together to speak in the responsible, measured tones of a soldier addressing his superior officers. When we arrived over the Chop Vum area, I noticed that the destruction of the houses had increased considerably. Most of the village of Phai Tay, inside the fork of the rivers, was now in ruins, and so were some additional houses to the east of the churches on the road running below Chop Vum. To the west of Chop Vum, a greater number of scattered individual houses had been destroyed than when I was last there, presumably by phosphorus rockets fired from helicopters, or by artillery fire. The high-flying white flag that had stood in front of the remains of one church was gone.

Captain Leroy had been given the coördinates of two pre-planned strikes, and these turned out to be situated on the southern and eastern flanks of the hill that had been evacuated by the command post on the first day of the operation. The southern flank was heavily wooded, and the first air strike, which consisted of both napalm and bombs, blew several gaping holes in the trees, but no further effect was visible. The eastern flank, a broad, gently inclined slope, was terraced at its based and wooded above that, except for the summit, which was blackened and bald, having been bombed and burned during the L.Z. prep. Halfway up the eastern flank, where the terraced fields came to an end, small paths curved up to several groups of three or four houses ranged around courtyards in small clearings in the woods. Starting at the base of the hill, Captain Leroy guided the F-4s up the slope, giving instructions to the pilots to "get those hootches." Napalm splashed on two groups of houses, and they immediately began to burn, but a number of napalm canisters landed far from their mark, and Captain Leroy was displeased with the performance as a whole.

As though to set things right, he announced to me, "O.K., now it's *my* turn to get me a hootch," and brought the plane into a dive and lined up in his front windshield a group of houses that were about three hundred yards from the original target area. He fired a rocket—the only one he had left—and white smoke puffed up about twenty yards from the houses. "Damn! Missed!" he exclaimed. But about thirty seconds later the houses burst into flames. "Hey, I got it!" he said, in a surprised voice. "It must be as dry as hell down there."

Three people ran out of one house and along a narrow path toward a line of trees, where they disappeared from sight. "Look! See those people?" Captain Leroy said. "They're running for their bunkers. See the bunkers where they're running to?"

He reported to Chu Lai that six military structures had been destroyed.

A minute later, I asked him if he judged that the people who had run out of the house were members of the Vietcong.

"All the innocent civilians have had a chance to get out

of here if they wanted to," he answered. "They're always warned. I saw a Psy War plane dropping leaflets."

I asked where all the civilians that had left had gone.

"Oh, they go to friends' houses—places like that," he said.

I remarked that there had been almost no people in sight on the roads since the operation began.

"They got out before the operation began," he said. "Look. Those villages are completely infested with V.C., just like rats' nests, and the only solution is to burn them out completely. That's the only way we can do it."

Captain Leroy continued to circle, watching the countryside below.

A few minutes later, a flight commander called him on the radio. "We've got some twenty mike-mike up here left over from another strike, and we wondered if you could use it anywhere," the pilot said.

"I'll check with the ground commander," Captain Leroy answered, and he did so, whereupon the ground commander said he would check with his unit commanders. Ten minutes later, he called back and said, "They don't have any place you can use it right now, but I wondered if you could put it on top of the old command post to explode any artillery shells that are still up there, so that the V.C. can't get them."

Captain Leroy directed the fighter-bombers to the target. The 20-mm.-cannon shells sparkled briefly on the hilltop as the planes made three passes, but there were no secondary explosions.

As Captain Leroy turned back to Chu Lai, his radio picked up a conversation on the ground.

A voice from a ground unit said, "We killed four V.C. this morning, sir. We turned around and saw that these guys were following us. They saw that we had spotted them, and we fired, and they took evasive action. We got all four of them, though. They didn't have weapons, but they were wearing the short V.C.-type black-pajama uniforms, and they were definitely of military age. No question about that, sir."

On the way back to the base, I asked Captain Leroy how the FAC pilots liked their assignment in Vietnam.

"At the beginning, they'd probably prefer to be zooming around in the F-4s, but after they get the FAC assignment, they like it all right. There's no complaining," he answered.

The next morning—the fifth day of Operation Benton—I flew on a mission with Major Billings. On the third day of the operation, elements of the 196th Light Infantry Brigade had been lifted into a valley east of the 1st of the 101st's area of operation and adjacent to it, in the hope of intercepting enemy units that might attempt to flee in that direction. We flew over this valley, and Major Billings pointed out what appeared to be a wisp of fog hanging over fields and houses. "See that haze down there?" he asked. "That's gas. It's not lethal, though—it just makes them nauseated, so they throw up, and generally puts them out of action. The troops were getting fire out of that area, so they put the gas in to clean the place out. Then the troops went in with gas masks."

When we arrived over the Chop Vum area, I saw that bombing, rocket fire, and artillery fire had destroyed more houses there. On the north side of the mountain, a dozen or more lines of smoke rose from the villages along the Song Tien—the usual sign that troops on the ground were burning houses. Presently, Major Billings flew over these villages, and I could tell from the smoke and ashes that at that point two dozen houses had been burned down.

Major Billings, weaving the plane back and forth to confuse the aim of snipers, brought us to below a hundred feet and made several passes over the burning villages. Families stood in their front yards watching their houses collapse in the flames. Some American troops stood in the yards next to the villagers, and others were pressing ahead through the trees, setting more houses on fire.

I asked Major Billings whether the men on the ground might not be annoyed with him if they knew he had brought a member of the press down low while they were burning a village.

"Oh, no! They *like* it!" he answered.

Major Billings flew out ahead of the troops and over the unburned part of the village and its fields. At one point, he said to me, "Look, here's what I want you to see—spider holes. They'll all be interconnected, and you will have a perfect position for Charlie to fire at our troops from here." He brought the plane down to fifty or sixty feet as we rushed over an embankment that had three or four black holes in it, spaced about ten yards apart. The fields were marked with craters, and several houses had been obliterated or half destroyed by artillery shells. A water buffalo lay dead on its side in the center of a rice field.

Major Billings' assignment for the day was to guide a pre-planned strike whose coördinates turned out to indicate the flat, broad top of a hill in the Chop Vum area. There were houses and crops on the hilltop and part way down the sides—until the slope became too steep for terracing. Ten or fifteen houses had already been destroyed, but on the very top—two rounded peaks, where the land was flat enough for a few rice fields—five or six large houses remained standing. Because the coördinates described the target only as a certain square a hundred metres on a side, the whole top of the hill, including patches of fields and woods, was included in the designation for the strike. Major Billings decided to concentrate the strike on the houses.

I asked him what type of target this was, and he said that he had been given only the coördinates, and no description, but that he guessed the most appropriate one would be "Suspected Enemy Troop Concentration," or else "Enemy Base Area."

A flight of F-4s arrived in the area, and the flight commander announced to Major Billings that they were carrying five-hundred-pound bombs, napalm, and 20-mm. cannon for strafing fire.

Major Billings brought our plane into a dive and fired a phosphorus rocket directly into the rice fields. One F-4 made a practice pass over the target, and the next F-4 began the air strike with two five-hundred-pound bombs. The pair of bombs exploded in the woods a hundred and fifty metres down the hill. The bombs from the second plane landed two hundred metres down the hill.

"They're nowhere *near* the target today," Major Billings said to me. Then, addressing the flight commander, he said, "Try and bring it up the hill some—about a hundred and fifty metres."

"Roger. Sorry," the flight commander answered.

The bombs from the next three passes landed between a hundred and a hundred and fifty metres away from the target area.

"Jesus, they haven't got one bomb anywhere near the target," Major Billings said to me. Then, adopting a patient tone, he told the flight commander, "The area I want you to hit is right up there next to my smoke, up where those hootches are."

"I see it," the flight commander answered. "I'll see if we can put these last loads on it."

Napalm canisters from the next two passes also landed down the hill in the woods. The canisters from a third pass tumbled down onto the hilltop, landing in one of the rice fields.

"Now you're on," said Major Billings. "Now try to lay twenty mike-mike across the same area."

When the heavy black cloud from the third load of napalm cleared above the rice fields, two houses were on fire. Their black frames showed briefly through the brilliant-orange flame and then crumpled. All three strafing passes cut across the fields and the houses, ending the strike. Soon two more houses burst into flame.

"I'm only going to give you twenty-per-cent Bombs on Target and fifty-per-cent Target Coverage," Major Billings told the flight commander. Then he radioed to the control desk at Chu Lai the information that four military structures had been destroyed.

With the strike over, Major Billings made a brief flight to the northern edge of the 1st of the 101st's area of operation, and beyond its borders I noticed the flames of burning houses and several lines of smoke rising from both sides of a small valley. The Major explained that the Marines had launched an operation named Cochise just to the north of Operation Benton and timed to coincide with it. We flew back over the Chop Vum area, and I found that the ground troops I had seen moving about north of the mountain had pressed about half a kilometre eastward, leaving a path of burned houses behind them.

As we were flying over Chop Vum, a unit commander

somewhere on the ground addressed a superior officer on the radio. "I've got an old lady here, sir. What should I do with her?" he asked.

"The important thing is to keep moving ahead here. Don't get bogged down with the refugee thing," the officer answered.

"Should I send her home again, or is there a safe area to send the people we find to?" the unit commander asked.

"No, there isn't, but the important thing is to steer clear of the refugee problem," the officer said. "Otherwise, you'll just get bogged down, like C Company did."

"Yes, sir," the unit commander said.

Major Billings turned back toward Chu Lai, and I asked him what percentage of the houses in the 1st of the 101st's area of operation he judged to have been destroyed during the first five days of Operation Benton.

He looked down at the landscape and answered, "Not half. Maybe forty per cent."

At the central control desk the next day, a captain compiled a report for me on the tonnage of explosives used, the number of air strikes carried out, and the results of the strikes during the first five days of Operation Benton in the area around Chop Vum that I had selected for observation at the beginning of the operation. I described the area to him in terms of its coördinates on the aviation maps, and for much of his information he drew on the Bomb Damage Assessment Reports, or B.D.A.s, turned in by the FAC pilots. The report reads:

5 DAYS/NIGHTS OPERATION BENTON
Partial Coverage of Base Area 117
 43 Strike Missions Actually Flown.
 20 of these with accountable B.D.A.
 23 of these with no B.D.A. due to heavy foliage, darkness, smoke

ACCOUNTABLE B.D.A. FOR 20 MISSIONS
139 Military Structures Destroyed
33 Military Structures Damaged
17 Military Bunkers Destroyed
3 Military Bunkers Damaged
4 Secondary explosions
125 metres Trenchwork destroyed
1 Tunnel Complex destroyed
1 Tunnel Destroyed
1 Automatic Weapon Position Silenced
1 Large Rice Field Destroyed

ORDNANCE EXPENDED

Bombs	Napalm Cans	Rockets
251	93	339
20-mm. Cannon		Flares
25,600 Rds.		145

7.62-mm. (miniguns)
21,200 Rds.

I was unable to determine the number of artillery rounds fired into the Chop Vum area, but two thousand and five rounds had been fired into the 1st of the 101st's whole area of operation, which was about ten kilometres on a side, and included the Chop Vum area. There was no damage assessment available for artillery fire, helicopter machine-gun fire, or phosphorus rockets, nor could I learn how many houses had been burned by troops on the ground.

D during my stay with the FAC pilots, they and other officers said again and again that we could win the war quickly if only we weren't under so many restraints. They spoke mainly of three kinds of restraints. First, they said that except where troops were engaged in battle, villages could not be bombed until the villagers had been warned by a leaflet drop or a loud-speaker announcement. Second, they said that when we wanted to turn an area into a "free-strike zone"—that is, an area in which we could bomb at will, and without warning —the villagers had to be evacuated. Third, they said that we could not destroy an area until we had cleared the action with the province chief. To find out about the warning system, I spoke with the Psychological Warfare Office for Task Force Oregon; to find out about evacuation I spoke with the Civil Affairs Office for the 101st Airborne Division; and to find out about the clearance system I spoke with the province chief. Having flown over Operation Benton during its first five days, I confined my inquiries to that operation in that period. All in all, my investigation disclosed that the procedures for applying these restraints were modified or twisted or ignored to such an extent that in practice the restraints evaporated entirely, though enough motions were gone through to create the illusion of restraints in the minds of the officers.

At the Task Force Oregon Psychological Warfare Office, the lieutenant colonel in charge told me that his people had dropped 1,515,000 leaflets over the area of operation and had made one announcement, but that all these had been of a very general nature, and none had warned of impending air strikes. He showed me a copy, in the original English, of each of the leaflets that had been dropped, including a group that the men at the Psychological Warfare Office refer to as "the Chieu Hoi mix" ("Chieu Hoi" means "Open Arms"), which consists of various leaflets encouraging members of the Vietcong to defect to the side of the G.V.N.—that is, the South Vietnamese Government. Some are threatening, showing photographs of the naked corpses of Vietcong soldiers riddled with bullet holes and heaped in piles, and others are conciliatory, showing photographs of smiling defectors along with signed statements saying that life in the government camps is prosperous and happy. The Psychological Warfare planes also dropped a hundred and eighty thousand copies of Leaflet No. 47-65, which is titled "Vietcong Mines Cause Senseless Deaths" and shows a cartoon drawing of several farmers reeling from an explosion in a rice field. The caption reads, "The V.C. mine your rice fields and cause you to go hungry. You must help the ARVN and the Marines to stop the Vietcong and deny the Vietcong any of your own rice." On the back is this text: "Vietcong mines kill Vietnamese on the roads, in the villages, and in the rice fields. Help your friends and neighbors by reporting such V.C. activities." Finally, they dropped a hundred thousand copies of Leaflet No. 167-66, which shows a cartoon drawing of a boorish Communist Chinese official laughing cruelly and spilling food all over a table as he eats a lavish meal while at his feet a moronic-looking Vietnamese with a Vietcong star on his tattered conical hat crouches under the table and picks up scraps of food from the floor. The text on the back reads:

APPEAL TO THE V.C. TO REJECT THE RED CHINESE AS THEIR MASTERS

The Red Chinese Communist masters of the Vietcong have declared that the South Vietnamese people must pay more and more to support the unjust war of the Vietcong. Still the Vietcong soldiers go hungry and they are not paid. Where does the rice and money go? Think about it! Refuse to give your rice and money—don't let the Chinese Communists make fools of you.

The colonel gave me a short briefing on the activities of his office over the previous three months. "We drop leaflets based on the desire to exploit their vulnerability," he told me. "We drop more than a million a day. We use mostly Cessna O-2s for the drops, but now we are getting in C-47s, and they can drop two million leaflets in one flight." (Later, I looked at the office notebook of leaflets—well over a thousand of them, of different types. The book is divided into "Campaigns," such as "Support G.V.N.," "V.C.," "Instructions to Civilians," "Chieu Hoi," and "Health." The "Health" leaflets give tips on personal and public hygiene. For example, they advise the villagers always to boil water before drinking it, to cover their garbage, and to sleep under mosquito nets. The leaflets usually end with the assurance that the G.V.N. "cares for the people.")

The colonel went on to say, "We also have a new aircraft that carries an eighteen-hundred-watt bank of loudspeakers effective up to five thousand feet. We've got several standard tapes that we can run off here. We played the national-reconciliation tape for a couple of hours over Benton. We make our own tapes here, too, using *hoi chanh*"—returnees, that is—"the way we do with the leaflets. Sometimes we play a tape *and* drop the leaflets. The *hoi chanh* tell how well they've been treated, and that kind of thing."

I asked what the national-reconciliation tape said.

"Well, I don't have a translation of the actual words, but the general idea is to get them to return to the government cause," the colonel said. "We get the targets for the different kinds of leaflets through intelligence and interrogation of *hoi chanh*. We try to cause disaffection between the top V.C. and the V.C. rank-and-file, and we advertise the Chieu Hoi Program. One of our big problems here is lack of support for the government, but this problem exists for the V.C., too. A lot of the people are in the V.C. because of force, and there are a lot in because it is the thing to do—because the neighbors are doing it. Last year, there were a hundred and sixteen defectors in Quang Ngai. I Corps, which includes Quang Ngai and four other northern provinces, has a high rate of defectors."

"Do you estimate the rate of defectors as the number of *hoi chanh* in the population of the province or as the number of *hoi chanh* in the estimated number of enemy troops in the area?" I asked.

"I don't know the precise details of how they measure it, but anyway it's very high here," the colonel answered, and he continued, "We've also got posters that we put up in the area. On the fourth of May, the V.C. blew up some houses at Ly Tra and Li Tinh, a few kilometres southeast of Tam Ky, in Quang Tin. So we made up some atrocity posters." The colonel got up from his desk to show me some large posters on an easel that stood at the back of his office. They featured photographs of the burned or blown-up bodies of women and children, and scenes of destroyed houses followed by scenes of Vietnamese reconstructing a village. The colonel, however, was not sure that the destruction of villages and the killing of villagers was always an unsound tactic on the part of the Vietcong, and after gazing gravely at the poster for a moment he smiled and said, "But the distribution of atrocity posters has to be limited. Sometimes they influence the people the wrong way, and help out the V.C. Sometimes it is just what the V.C. want."

The colonel then said that many ground units were aided by loudspeaker teams who broadcast ahead of the American troops, encouraging the enemy to surrender. In combat, the Psychological Warfare Officers preferred to play tapes rather than use live voices. "That way, the guy is sure to sound confident, and we avoid fluttery, scared-sounding voices," the colonel explained. "Sometimes they use the tapes to broadcast from the perimeter of the U.S. troops. Mostly, we play music and interrupt it with what we call our commercials. We use nostalgic music to make the V.C. feel lonesome and want to go back home. We know from research that flute music is nostalgic to the Vietnamese. We've got three main pieces—one with a man, one with a woman, and one with a flute. The man and the woman sing of their lovely home. The Vietnamese are very closely related to their land. There is an old Vietnamese legend about a commander who was so good on the flute that all the enemy dropped their weapons and went home when he played it. We haven't had that happen yet. But I want to emphasize that in all our leaflets and pamphlets we *tell only the truth*. This is, of course, to establish our credibility, so that the people can depend completely on the truth of what we say."

I pointed out that we had destroyed about forty per cent of the houses in the Benton area of operation during its first five days, and asked him how he viewed this.

"We do destroy villages, and we have to," he answered. "But there are rules of engagement that prevent us from just arbitrarily bombing any friendly village. Whenever there's time, we get a Psy War bird out there to warn them. That way, we keep from hurting as many civilians as we can. Also, when the V.C. set off a mine in the road, and someone innocent gets killed, the V.C. exploit us and say, 'See what the American artillery has done!' So we drop our standard leaflets about V.C. mines."

The colonel also told me about units called audio-visual teams, which showed movies in the camps and villages when they got a chance. "They show American films, usually—mostly Westerns," he said. "Once, they showed 'The Swinger.' That wasn't too good. That was a mistake. They won't show that one again. But we try to show pictures that portray the American way of life. We're careful to show them things they understand. For instance, if you show them a science-fiction movie, they won't know what's going on. Walt Disney pictures are good, because the words aren't too important. In between reels, we show cartoons and shorts that liberally assert our propaganda. A lot of these are made by the South Vietnamese Ministry of Information. One shows a North Vietnamese soldier goofing up—falling into a canal, and that kind of thing. Another shows how a *hoi chanh* decided to defect. Sometimes we get the village chief to address the people between reels. You see, they don't have any TV or movies or record-players, or anything. So when we show them something, they gobble it right up. What we are accomplishing is to leave a good taste in the mouths of the children, so that when they grow up and the V.C. try to persuade them they'll remember the nice things the Allies did for them."

As I passed out of the colonel's private office into a larger room, which was filled with the desks of other Psychological Warfare Officers, a captain was calling out to a lieutenant, "Hey, Ray, what about a nice nostalgic tape by a woman?"

"Fine!" answered the lieutenant. He was peering at the Psychological Warfare Office target map, which was enclosed in a folder decorated on the outside with two *Playboy* Playmates of the Month.

A minute later, the captain handed the lieutenant the English original of a leaflet to read.

The lieutenant objected that a curfew that was announced in the leaflet should read, "From sundown to sunrise," instead of "From 6:00 P.M. to 6:00 A.M." "The

Vietnamese don't know what time it is," the lieutenant said. "They don't have any watches."

"Sure they do," the captain replied. "You look around the bases and you'll see they've all got watches."

"Yeah, on the bases," the lieutenant said. "But you go out on Route 1, where they're carrying wood and rice and stuff, and I'll give you a double mixed drink for every watch you see."

"All I know is we announced the last curfew by the hours," said the captain, and the two men moved on to another question.

A chart on the wall next to the captain's desk showed in one column the number of leaflets dropped each month so far in 1967, in a second column the number of defectors for each month, and in a third column the number of defectors for each month of 1966. The captain told me, "We keep tables on how many defectors we get every month to gauge how effective we've been, and we feel pretty good about the fact that we've had more *hoi chanh* this year than in the same months last year, because this is where we measure the results. This is where we can see we are really doing something." There was, however, no correspondence between the number of leaflets dropped during the months of Task Force Oregon's operations and the number of defectors in those months.

I visited a small tent serving as the Civil Affairs Office of the 1st Brigade of the 101st Division, to ask how many people had been evacuated from the Benton area of operation, and learned that Operation Benton was not supposed to "generate any new refugees." Apparently, word that the camps had been able to provide care—and then only minimal care—for only a fraction of the area's dispossessed people had reached Saigon, and Task Force Oregon had been requested to conduct operations in a way

that would not result in a great increase in the number of
people arriving at the camps. During the first week of
Operation Benton, Task Force Oregon's solution to the
problem was to conduct the operation as usual but omit
the step of evacuating the villagers, either before or after
their villages were destroyed. I learned this when, on the
sixth day of the operation, I asked the major in charge of
the Civil Affairs Office how many of the seventeen thousand people who lived in the area of operation had been
evacuated, and he told me that fifteen people had been
lifted out by helicopter and that a hundred more were
waiting for transportation. I pointed out that about forty
per cent of the houses in the area had already been destroyed without any warning to the villagers, and the
major told me that, with the help of the Psychological
Warfare Office, the Civil Affairs Office had devised a more
flexible plan, which would be put into action during the
second week of the operation; this was intended to offer
the inhabitants of the area what the major described as a
"free choice" between going to the government camps and
remaining on the sites of their homes. Each American
soldier would be given a handful of leaflets designed ex-
pressly for Operation Benton, and would himself pass
them out to the people of the area when his commanding
officer instructed him to do so. The leaflet to be employed—No. 244-133-68—was titled "Move to Ly Tra
Refugee Camp," and read:

> The American soldier who handed you this
> is here to help you free yourself from the Viet-
> cong and the North Vietnamese invaders who
> bring upon you the ravages of war. He will
> take you and your family to Ly Tra, where the
> G.V.N. will protect you. There you can live a

peaceful, prosperous life without fear for the lives of your beloved ones. You will go to Ly Tra by helicopter and will be able to take only the personal possessions you carry. The G.V.N. has a refugee center at Ly Tra that will give you aid until you can reëstablish yourself.

If you desire to go to Ly Tra, touch the American soldier on his shoulder. He will understand. Get your belongings together and follow the American's instructions. If you do not wish to go to Ly Tra, tear this leaflet in half. He will understand that you do not wish to go.

I asked the major in charge of the Civil Affairs Office what he thought the purpose of Operation Benton was.

"The province chief has told us this is pretty much a hundred-per-cent V.C. area," he answered. "We consider just about everything here to be a hard-core V.C., or at least some kind of supporter. Before they bomb an area, a Psy War bird always goes in ahead. This is an operation to catch the V.C., not to clear the area. You can't just go around moving everybody out all the time."

I asked if the Civil Affairs Office had any further plans for the people in the region.

"Now you're getting out of our area," he answered. "*We* don't have any plans for the immediate future. It's the responsibility of the G.V.N. and the ARVN to carry out Pacification and Revolutionary Development."

While we stood talking, a captain at a desk nearby received a phone call, and after he hung up he said to the major, "That was the colonel, and he wants those two villages burned. He said the province chief requested it."

A tall young lieutenant in fatigues and an undershirt,

on the other side of the tent, interrupted the conversation to ask, "What about the people?"

"The colonel said we're not supposed to bring out any refugees," the captain replied.

"What do you mean? How can we burn a village if we're not going to bring out the people?"

"Well, those are the colonel's orders."

"Look," the lieutenant said, standing up. "We have our rules of engagement, and we can't just go around burning villages without taking care of the people. That's just ridiculous! Can you have any respect for a colonel who gives an order like that? I mean, no kidding—can you?"

"The province chief ordered us to do it," the captain said.

The lieutenant sat down again.

A sergeant from the Operations Office spoke up to say, "The Vietnamese can relocate themselves. That's the way they are. Every two years or so, they'll just pick up their sticks and move on to somewhere else on their own. That's the way it was in Korea, too. The villages got wiped out there, too, and everybody just picked up their stuff and went somewhere else. Those aren't houses. They're just huts. Take, for instance, all those people who came down from North Vietnam for religious reasons. The North is Catholic and the South is Buddhist. That's one reason why they don't like each other." Actually, of course, both North Vietnam and South Vietnam are predominantly Buddhist, with a Catholic minority.

The next day, I drove to Tam Ky, the capital of Quang Tin Province, to see Lieutenant Colonel Hoang Dinh Tho, who is the Province Chief, and ask him about his role in providing clearance for Task Force Oregon's activities for the first five days of Operation Benton and in his province generally. His office was in a large two-story building in the ornate, pastel-colored colonial French style, which stood in a large courtyard at the end of a long driveway lined with trees, on the outskirts of Tam Ky. At the entrance to the driveway, two three-story modern-style stucco towers stood like giant bookends on a plain that had had its trees bulldozed away for security. There was a guardhouse beside one of the towers, and beyond them coils of barbed wire stretched out into brown fields. A Vietnamese officer there explained to me that an arch was to have stretched between the towers but that materials had run out. He said that the trees had been planted as a special project in an effort that President Diem had made to beautify the country. Flanking the office of the Province Chief were two long, low buildings occupied by officers of the ARVN and their American advisers. Just as I arrived—it was shortly after noon—a pickup truck pulled up to one of these buildings. In the back of the truck, an American soldier holding a shotgun guarded about twenty Vietnamese, whose heads were covered with muddy sandbags. In their blindness, some had clasped hands and others had their arms around each other. A Vietnamese officer shouted something to them, and they removed the bags and looked about them, blinking in the whitish noon sun. Five of them were young women, eight or nine were young or middle-aged men, three were old men, and two were young girls with still boyish figures. When they had helped each other climb shakily off the truck, they were delivered into the hands of a tall, young, collegiate-looking American soldier with a shock of straight dark hair, who appeared to be intensely irritated by something. "Get over there!" he shouted to the people, pointing with a sheaf of papers he was holding toward one end of the building. The people looked in the direction he indicated but did not move. "I said *get moving!*" the young soldier shouted, and struck an old man—who happened to be standing near him—in the face with his sheaf of papers. The old man fell back, his gaze riveted on the young American, who then turned away and stalked ahead of the group, his face red and furious. Four American officers who had been standing on a porch talking and watching the prisoners get off the truck went inside the building. The people filed around a corner of the building and were led toward a small, white-washed, windowless structure that stood alone in a withered field. Several ARVN officers who had been loung-ing outside it began to pick themselves up sluggishly as the people came in sight.

I asked an American officer passing through the square who the Vietnamese prisoners were.

"Detainees," he answered. "They picked them up back in the mountains somewhere, and now they're taking them out back for interrogation." (Several times during my stay in Quang Ngai and Quang Tin, I saw groups of detainees, always with sandbags over their heads, being herded into airplanes or trucks under the guard of Americans carrying shotguns. I learned at the Task Force Oregon Information Office that ninety-three per cent of them were eventually cleared as innocent and released.)

In due course, I was received by Colonel Tho, who is about forty and is shorter than most of his countrymen. He has strikingly clear and handsome features, he was im-maculately groomed, and he displayed a solid, if inelegant, command of English, which he had acquired during two years of military training in the United States. It had recently been reported in the Vietnamese military press that Colonel Tho had insisted that several air-conditioners intended for his own spacious offices be installed in an ARVN hospital instead. I mentioned this to him when I met him, and he laughed in delight and embarrassment, brushing the matter away with a sweep of his hand. Colonel Tho then motioned to an American officer standing behind him, who stepped forward for a few seconds to introduce himself, in a hushed voice, as Lieutenant Colonel Robert O. Lynch, Senior Adviser for Quang Tin Province, and then stepped back, solemn-faced, like a well-trained butler. Throughout the interview, Colonel Tho laughed often and gesticulated expansively, and Colonel Lynch sat silent, apparently to avoid cramping the Province Chief's style with an overbearing American presence.

We sat down around a small coffee table, and I asked Colonel Tho what his role had been in the planning of Operation Benton, and whether he had restrained Task Force Oregon from any bombings or shellings during the first five days of the operation. I learned that his method of giving clearance in an American military operation was not to review the targets of individual air strikes or shellings but to give the American ground commander a blanket clearance before the operation was launched. The Chop Vum area had been covered by such a clearance, and Colonel Tho had received no information on the results of any American air strikes, except in terms of enemy casualties, since the beginning of Operation Benton.

"The American Army comes to me to ask my permission for running the operation, and I tell them the areas they can't bomb," Colonel Tho told me. Later, I learned that he had been called to a meeting two days before the operation and had been asked to specify the no-strike zones. It had then been agreed not to operate within several kilometres of the town of Phuoc Tien. "Outside of Phuoc Tien, the ground commander decides where to bomb," he went on. "Sometimes I give permission to burn a fortified village on the ground, but not so many in this operation. Just one or two. Sometimes the villages support the V.C., and they are *too strong*, so they must be destroyed."

I asked him about his plans for the civilians in the area.

"No refugees this time, unless they *ask* to come," Colonel Tho said. "We take out only villagers who are friendly to protect in the government area. For relatives of the V.C., maybe they have to suffer some."

At this point, Colonel Lynch looked up, and, after asking and receiving the Province Chief's permission to speak, he said, "Of course, when we *do* have to destroy a village, in almost every case we warn the people in advance with announcements or leaflets. We're very careful about that."

I asked Colonel Tho if there were any plans for securing the area after Operation Benton was over.

"Well, maybe, sometime, but now we don't have enough troops," Colonel Tho said. "This operation is just to get the main-force V.C. units. This war has many faces. Sometimes we find V.C., and move some people for economic war. Sometimes economic war is most important. Population control. Change the population patterns."

I observed to the Province Chief that the two churches in Thanh Phuoc had been bombed, and asked if he had heard about that.

"Oh, yes," he said. "I got the report this morning that V.C.s blow up two churches."

I said that I had seen American planes bomb the churches.

The Province Chief laughed for several seconds, and said, "Well, in the fighting you cannot always tell what is happening, and you cannot always tell the difference between just regular houses and church."

Later, I spoke with a captain in the ARVN who had been in and out of the northern provinces since the end of the Second World War, and he expressed alarm at the policies that our military had developed in I Corps over the past year or so. "The Americans are destroying everything," he said. "If they get just one shot from a village, they destroy it. We have an expression: The American S-5 builds a village and the American S-3 destroys it." S-5 is the Civil Affairs Office, and S-3 is the Operations Office. "I helped give out rice and building materials in one village, and three days later it was completely bombed. They bomb villages with the families of our troops living in them. A soldier comes back from Saigon and finds that his family has been killed. They bomb the rich and the poor. The rich man is the V.C.'s enemy. We should protect him. But now he has two enemies: the V.C., and the Americans who bomb all the houses. They even bomb the houses of the local militia. Who has made this new policy? The Americans never try to protect a village. Just one V.C.—*just one*—can enter any village with a machine gun and the people are helpless against him. What can they do? Nothing. He shoots, and then their village is bombed."

On my way back to Chu Lai from Tam Ky, I had an opportunity to talk for fifteen minutes or so with several members of a group of about a hundred civilians who had been brought to a staging area from the Benton area of operation the day before. According to plans worked out by the office of the Province Chief, villagers who might be brought out of the area would enter the government camp at Ly Tra, but when the officials at Ly Tra heard about this they refused to accept any new arrivals, declaring that they already had far more people than they could supply with food and shelter. The evacuated villagers were split up and shunted off to a number of smaller camps. The jeep I was riding in happened to stop at the staging area. The hundred-odd villagers, who were from several different parts of the Benton area, were grouped on a concrete platform the size of half a basketball court, which was covered by a tin roof mounted on metal stilts. The platform stood in the center of a vast, treeless, sandy, scrubby expanse. There was a good deal of this type of terrain on the shore side of Route 1 in Quang Tin and Quang Ngai, but it had not traditionally been a living place for the Vietnamese; they had always built their houses near trees and water, and had reserved the arid fields of white sand and coarse grasses as sites for tombs. Next to the platform stood several rows of huts with roofs of tin or thatch and walls of straw or cardboard. These housed people who had left their homes earlier in the year.

There were no Americans at the site, but, with the aid of an interpreter, I discovered that a group of people who had lived around the two bombed churches in Thanh Phuoc were present. I approached this group, and attempted to address myself to a young woman who was crouching on the concrete with three children holding on to her, but this proved impossible, for ten or twelve other people immediately crowded around me and all answered my questions at once. The interpreter was overwhelmed by the hail of answers, and succeeded in interpreting no more than a fraction of them. There were only two or three young men in the entire assemblage of civilians, but there were quite a lot of old women, and they were by far the boldest in speaking out. I asked the group around me where they had gone when the bombing began, and I received a hail of answers.

"We went in our caves."

"We didn't come out for three days. We ran out of food."

"I want to go back to find my sister."

"My house was bombed."

"We don't have anything to eat here."

"Three people were killed."

"Can I have some rice?"

"We don't have any blankets here."

"All the houses were bombed."

"We hid in the caves and brought the children."

"We couldn't bring any possessions."

I asked whether they had been able to reach the camp with their families intact.

"I am thankful to say that all my children are here."

"I don't know where my daughter is."

"My daughters are here, but my son is gone."

"My husband isn't here."

"We couldn't bring anything."

"I want to go back to find my father."

I was apparently the first American who had spoken to them, and they naturally mistook me for someone in charge, who could help them. When one woman said she wanted to go back to find other members of her family, there was an immediate outburst of enthusiasm from the group.

"Will you send the helicopters back to bring more people?"

"Can I go back?"

"I don't have any food."

"Will you bring out more people?"

When they asked me to send helicopters back for their

relatives, some of the villagers pointed to the blue mountains on the edge of the hot plain.

The men present did not answer unless they were addressed specifically. Upon being asked about his family, one old man, who was wearing a pith helmet and the black pàjamalike garment that most Vietnamese farmers wear, told me with exaggerated politeness that his son was an ARVN soldier, and immediately several women chorused that they, too, had sons in the ARVN.

"My son went into the ARVN four years ago and I haven't heard anything from him since," another woman added.

"My son went with the Vietcong," said still another.

Some of the women, apparently not putting much trust in my interpreter, resorted to gestures and pantomime to gain my attention. They stretched out empty palms to show that they had nothing, pointed to dirty children or pointed to their stomachs, and made theatrically exaggerated piteous faces, mimicking their own suffering. One woman grabbed me by the sleeve and tugged me a few yards to a tiny pile of clothes and blackened pots, and told me, "This is all I could bring."

Among the people assembled on the platform were some who stood with glazed eyes and parted lips. I asked a woman about one of these, and she answered, "He has a fever. Many of the other people have fevers." She shook her head and said, "It is not good to have a fever."

Several other people took no interest in my presence, and one young mother, who was squatting barefoot among her children, turned her back with a sorrowful, angry look when I addressed her through my interpreter.

Children from the nearby huts had mingled with the newly arrived people, and these children were extremely bold. In the manner of most Vietnamese children who have lived anywhere near Americans for very long, they thrust their hands in my pockets and shouted "Chop-chop souvenir!" (which means, in effect, "Give me something to eat!"), or "Chewing gum! Chewing gum!," or simply "O.K.! O.K.! O.K.!" But four children from the Chop Vum area whom I attempted to talk to ran away and, when I followed them, would not meet my gaze.

After I had spoken with the people from Thanh Phuoc, I was approached by a thin middle-aged man in clean black clothes, who introduced himself as a former pastor of one of the two bombed churches. He said that he himself had left Thanh Phuoc a year and a half before, and had now come to the staging area to help settle the new arrivals. One of the churches had been Catholic and the other Protestant, he explained, and the people of Thanh Phuoc had built both churches themselves, about a decade earlier, under the guidance of missionary groups from Saigon, which had made the materials available.

As we drove away, a helicopter landed and a fatherless family climbed out onto the bare field, each person carrying a small bundle.

On August 27th, the day before Operation Benton was brought to a close, I flew on one more FAC mission over the Chop Vum area to see what had happened to it during the remainder of the operation. I flew with Captain Reese. As we crossed the 196th Light Brigade's area of operation, Captain Reese pointed out an avenue of brown trees and fields that was about two hundred yards wide and ran for three kilometres down the center of a cultivated valley. He explained that Operation Ranch Hand had sprayed the valley with defoliants three days earlier. As we approached the Chop Vum area, I found that during the nine days since I had last flown over the region about fifty per cent of the houses in the villages just north of the Song Tien had been destroyed. To judge by the appearance of the ruins and the density of the craters, the houses had been destroyed by bombing and artillery. In some places, a single house stood untouched in the center of a scene of devastation; in other places the ruins of a destroyed house lay in the center of an untouched group of houses. On the south side of the Song Tien, where ground troops had been burning houses when I last flew over the area, the houses had been systematically burned in a path that curved around to the eastern side of Chop Vum. Approximately sixty-five per cent of the houses in the Chop Vum area as a whole had been destroyed.

Captain Reese had been assigned to guide two preplanned strikes during his three-hour mission that day. On our way to the first target, I noticed five or six people on the roads and in the fields. When Captain Reese spotted three people in a rice field, he said to me, "They're down there around their houses, harvesting the rice. They oughta know better'n that. They're liable to get hurt." A minute later, having spotted a lone figure walking along a road, he said, "There's some guy. He probably lives here."

Over our radio, someone on the ground said, addressing someone else on the ground, "I went over, found a couple of people in the open, and took a couple of shots at them. They went away."

Another voice said, "We've got some suspects here. A couple of them look a little *old,* but the others look real good."

"Keep them for us," said an answering voice, with a heavy French accent. Captain Reese explained that the Intelligence Officer of one company was a former Frenchman who had fought with his countrymen in Vietnam before their defeat in 1954.

The first target turned out to be a patch of forest that was bordered on two sides by fields and houses. Someone walked quickly from a yard into a house as our plane approached.

Captain Reese asked a ground commander who was two or three kilometres away which part of the woods to bomb.

"Why don't you pick the best area for exfiltration?" the ground commander suggested.

"I really like that little knoll over to the west where you can see the exfiltration trails in the woods there," Captain Reese said. "I think we can expose it for you."

Just then, another ground commander interrupted to request an immediate strike. That afternoon, he explained, C Company was going to be landed by helicopter on a bare hill that stood among wooded hills and vegetable fields in the Chop Vum area. He gave Captain Reese the coördinates, and we flew to the designated place. Then Captain Reese asked the second ground commander if he wanted to have any particular spot hit.

"Well, C Company is going in there, and we want to give them preparation in any likely areas of enemy troop concentration," the ground commander answered.

"Well, I can see a valley that might be good, and another hill with some trails running up into the woods. Which place do you want?"

"Both of those places sound good to me. Pick the one y*ou* want."

"O.K. I think I'll put it in on the little hill. There's some trails going up there, and there might be something up there," Captain Reese said. He was looking down at a small, steep hill that was already marked with five or six large bomb craters. After checking for clearance, he waited for the fighter-bombers, and when they arrived he brought our plane into a dive and fired a phosphorus rocket. The puff of white smoke appeared about thirty yards from the summit of the hill.

The target was small, but in the ensuing air strike the fighter-bombers succeeded in sending three loads of bombs and one of napalm almost directly on the phosphorus smoke. Two final loads of napalm landed within fifty yards of the smoke.

When the strike was finished, Captain Reese congratulated the pilots on their unusually excellent aim. Then he made several low passes over the smoking hill, and remarked to me, "There ain't nothin' there."

Captain Reese turned back toward the first of his preplanned targets but was once again interrupted by a ground commander who wished to request an immediate strike. His company was operating about three kilometres north of the Song Tien and one kilometre north of a small road that ran east and west, parallel to the river. Instead of giving coördinates, the ground commander guided Captain Reese to the target by describing it in relation to landmarks on the ground.

"It's five hundred metres east of that pagoda on the road there. Have you got the pagoda?" the ground commander asked.

Captain Reese flew over the road from west to east for a minute, and answered, "I see a church but no pagoda."

"It's right under you now," the ground commander said.

"I don't see it," Captain Reese said.

"O.K., well, there's one hootch down there about a klik south of us that we want you to get," the ground commander said. "Klik" is military slang for a kilometre. "We've got sniper fire out of that tree line."

Captain Reese flew over the area indicated, and found

that it was occupied by a village of sixty or seventy houses. Many of the houses that remained standing here and elsewhere along the road now had white flags flying on poles in their front yards. "I see a village down there," he said.

"No, this is just one hootch," said the ground commander, who was apparently unable to see the village from his spot on the ground because of a thick cover of trees.

"Well, I'll put in a marker round," Captain Reese said, and he sent the plane into a dive. He bore down on the village and fired a phosphorus rocket into its center. "How's that?" he asked the ground commander as he brought the plane out of the dive.

"No, that's not it," the ground commander said. "I'm talking about that *one* hootch in the tree line over to the east a couple of hundred metres."

"I'll put in another rocket," Captain Reese said.

The second rocket exploded to the east of the first rocket but—from the point of view of the ground unit—several hundred yards behind it.

"That's the general area," said the ground commander, apparently tired of trying to pinpoint the one house.

"Do you want us to pretty well cover this general area?" Captain Reese asked.

"Affirmative. Hit the whole area. We've seen activity all through this area."

"The activity I see down there is all Charlie—is that right?"

"Roger. We're the only friendlies around."

"O.K., I'll put in a can of napalm and see what it looks like," Captain Reese said. Addressing the flight commander of three F-4s that had arrived overhead during the conversation with the ground commander, he said,

"Would you put your napes on those hootches down there, about a hundred yards from my smoke at ten o'clock."

"Roger," the flight commander answered. "I'll make my dry run now."

Shortly afterward, an F-4 cut through an opening in some large, puffy white clouds that were floating in a clear blue sky, and made a pass over the village.

"O.K., I've found a hole I can come down through onto the target," the pilot said.

On his next pass, the pilot sent two canisters of napalm down onto the western edge of the village. Two houses were immediately incinerated.

"Real fine. A real good hit," said Captain Reese.

The second plane sent its napalm into some vegetable fields next to the village. The napalm burned furiously in the brown earth and belched black smoke for about a half a minute. The napalm from the next pass again landed on the edge of the village, setting another house on fire.

"Yeah, yeah, yeah!" exclaimed Captain Reese.

"We've got two seven-hundred-fifty-pound bombs for this next run," the flight commander announced.

On the next pass, the two bombs landed in the vegetable fields, with the result that two small fields were eliminated by deep craters, and dirt was sprayed over the adjacent fields.

"We sure put some holes in their rice paddies there, didn't we?" Captain Reese remarked to me.

"Where do you want the strafe?" the flight commander asked.

Captain Reese referred the question to the ground commander.

"Try to get that one hootch," said the ground commander, who had not seen the results of the strike so far, because of the trees blocking his view.

"We'll try to get that hootch for you," Captain Reese said. "Shall we pretty much cover the area?"

"That's a roger," the ground commander said. "Any civilians in this area are Charlies, or Charlie sympathizers, so there's no sweat there."

"We'll work around through there with the twenty mike-mike," said Captain Reese. Addressing the flight commander, he said, "We'd like you to work around through this whole area." Then, apparently bringing his attention back to the problem of hitting the specific house that the ground commander was interested in but that the Captain himself had never identified, he seemed to decide, upon seeing a house with an especially large roof, that that was it. He said to the flight commander, "I'd like you to get that one big hootch north of where that first nape went in."

"The one with the big roof?" asked the flight commander.

"That's it," Captain Reese answered, not bothering to specify which of several big-roofed houses he had in mind—perhaps because any of them might have been the one the ground commander wanted destroyed.

The first strafing pass cut a sparkling path across the entire village. Three fairly big holes appeared in the red tile roof of a large stone house on its western edge. In back of this house, a tall palm tree was cut cleanly in half by one of the explosive shells, and its leafy top half slammed violently into a nearby yard.

"That's not the hootch I was thinking of," Captain Reese said. "Try to get the big one with a brown grass roof in the tree line to the right of it."

"Roger," answered the flight commander.

"Did you see that palm tree go down?" Captain Reese asked me. "That's how powerful those shells are."

On the next pass, the strafing fire cut across the entire village once again, this time drawing a flashing line through the large thatch-roofed house that Captain Reese had described to the flight commander. The house burst into flames, and a person ran out. Then two more people ran out, and then they all ran in again, to emerge once more, still at a run, with bundles in their arms. For about a minute, three or four people ran in and out of the house, bringing out bundles. Then the entire house was aflame and the roof fell in. As Captain Reese circled over the house, he watched the running people and remarked, "They're really gettin' it outta there. I don't blame them." Then, as though addressing the people carrying their belongings out of the house, he added, "Git it outta there! Git it outta there!"

When the house had collapsed entirely in the flames, Captain Reese headed away from the village and called the central control desk at Chu Lai. "We destroyed an Enemy Sniper Position. Seven structures were destroyed," he said in his Bomb Damage Assessment Report. After that, he asked the ground commander, "Did we get that hootch you wanted?"

"Well, you pretty much covered that whole area," the ground commander said.

The flight commander radioed to ask, "Did we get any K.B.A.s?"

"There's probably some K.B.A.s there," Captain Reese said. "We hit a hootch that they saw some snipers running into, but the ground unit probably won't go in there to look for bodies. That was real good work. I appreciate it."

"Well, thank you," the flight commander replied. "I enjoyed it."

Before returning to Chu Lai, Captain Reese had to

perform a final task—that of observing a "Will Adjust" artillery mission. The target was a patch of forest next to a rice field in which thirty or forty water buffalo stood grazing. A fence near one edge of the field had been intended to restrict the water buffalo to a narrow strip of it, but the buffalo had made a breach in the fence and were feeding on the rows of rice shoots.

"We're gonna scatter some cattle down there," said Captain Reese.

The first round of artillery was a smoke shell, and it landed in a field some three hundred yards short of the target. Captain Reese advised the battery, which was about ten kilometres away, of the degree of its error, and the next round, which was an explosive shell, landed some fifty yards from the target. The next salvo, which consisted of several explosive shells, landed in the target area. The water buffalo lifted their heads together to look at the smoke from the explosion, and then moved to the opposite edge of the field. At that point, another FAC plane arrived to guide the rest of the artillery mission, and Captain Reese headed our plane back to Chu Lai.

On one wall of their quarters, the FAC pilots had pinned a chart listing the K.B.A.s that were credited to missions guided by the various pilots in the past week. Major Billings was credited with four "points," Major Nugent with three, Captain Reese with four, Captain Leroy with two, and Lieutenant Moore with eleven. "Moore's got all the K.B.A.s," Major Billings remarked that evening. At the bottom of the chart, a carefully hand-lettered explanation of the point system read:

POINTS AS FOLLOWS:

MEN	WOMEN
old 3	old 3
crippled 3	crippled 3
children 3	children 3
military age 1	military age 1
	pregnant 5

Special this month: combination of two or more may also be counted.

In actuality, of course, the pilots rarely knew the age or sex of the people killed in air strikes, and this chart, like their joking at dinner the week before, seemed intended to ridicule the idea that innocent people were often killed by the bombings.

While I was looking at the chart, Major Nugent approached me with a troubled look and, shaking his head in disgust, said in a low voice, "Yeah, well, you know a couple of days ago a unit on the ground got some sniper fire from a hootch, so they called some phosphorus rockets on it. Then the guys on the ground rushed the place, and when they got there, there was nothing but two women and four kids in the hootch, all messed up real bad with shrapnel and phosphorus, and the V.C. had just plain disappeared. They couldn't find them anywhere, or find out where they went. That's the kind of war it is. That's what we're up against. Maybe those women were shooting. I don't know. It's the civilians who always get it. They get it in every war."

On August 28th, when Operation Benton came to a close, Task Force Oregon announced that the troops taking part in it had killed, and counted the bodies of, three hundred and ninety-seven of the enemy, and that forty-seven American soldiers had been killed. Into an area of ten by twenty kilometres they had dropped 282 tons of "general-purpose" bombs and 116 tons of napalm; fired 1,005 rockets (not counting rockets fired from helicopters), 132,820 rounds of 20-mm. explosive strafing shells, and 119,350 7.62-mm. rounds of machine-gun fire from Spooky flights; and fired 8,488 artillery rounds. By the end of the operation, the Civil Affairs Office had supervised the evacuation of six hundred and forty of the area's seventeen thousand people, to the vicinity of government camps.

The reports that were sent back to Saigon to form the over-all statistical picture of the war could be divided into two kinds. One kind measured the achievements of the American efforts in Vietnam in terms of materials expended—whether these were bombs dropped, artillery shells fired, Psychological Warfare leaflets dropped, pounds of rice distributed, or gallons of defoliants sprayed. Like the Psychological Warfare Officer for Task Force Oregon at Chu Lai who was encouraged by the fact that his people had stepped up the rate of leaflets dropped over Quang Ngai Province to a million a day, and like the artillery officer in Duc Pho who took pride in the fact that his men had fired sixty-four thousand and forty-four shells into two districts in three and a half months, most American officers and officials found cause for optimism in the sheer scale of the outputs of our efforts. The other kind of statistical report measured American achievements in Vietnam in terms of some of the effects of all this activity. The Bomb Damage Assessment Reports filled out by the FAC pilots were a good example. The terms "Military Structure," "Suspected Enemy Troop Concentration," "Percentage of Target Destroyed," and "Percentage of Bombs on Target," which described the bombing targets and the bomb damage, were devised by higher-ups, and the FAC pilots' only track-keeping duty was to write figures into the blanks. With this system, only results of the kind we intended to bring about were reported to Saigon, and the vast "side effects," such as the destruction of villages in large areas, went unmentioned. It is perhaps not very surprising that the Bomb Damage Assessment Reports supplied no blanks for "Homes Destroyed" or "Civilians Killed."

A further problem was that the terms employed in the Bomb Damage Assessment Reports often did not correspond to what the FAC pilots saw on the ground. When a FAC pilot guided an air strike onto a target that was defined by his coördinates only as a patch of jungle a hundred metres square, and was termed a "Suspected Enemy Troop Concentration," or guided an air strike onto a village that was described as an "Enemy Sniper Position," there was no meaning in a figure for the "Percentage of Target Destroyed," and little meaning in a figure for the "Percentage of Bombs on Target." Since the pilots could never know how much of the real target—the enemy troops—had been destroyed, they fell back on simply reporting how many houses had been destroyed, or how much of the hundred-metre-square patch of jungle had been torn up, as though this had been the objective of the bombing. Also, since the enemy was fighting primarily a guerrilla war, and built virtually no "military structures," the FAC pilots came to apply this term to any building that the planes happened to bomb. (Some of the bunkers and caves used by both the N.L.F. and the civilians might accurately have been called "military structures," but the Bomb Damage Assessment Reports listed these in a separate category.) Most of the terms used in the Bomb Damage Assessment Reports seemed to have been devised for something like a bombing raid on a large, clearly visible, stationary military base, and not for the bombing of guerrilla forces in the setting of fields, villages, and jungle which the FAC pilots actually guided. Finding himself having to guide air strikes with the aid of a set of instructions that had little relevance to his actual task, each FAC pilot had to improvise his own ways of trying to tell where the enemy was operating. This was how Captain Reese came to think that he could spot, on the trails, grass that had been freshly bent by the passage of enemy troops, and that he could distinguish enemy houses from civilian houses by whether they were in the tree lines or not; how Lieutenant Moore came to think that he could tell a farmer from a soldier by the way he walked; and how Major Billings came to believe that he could tell enemy soldiers from civilians by making a low pass over the fields and seeing who ran for cover, and that he could judge whether a wisp of smoke hanging over the woods was rising from the fire of a Montagnard or from the fire of a Vietcong soldier.

While some units of the 196th Light Infantry Brigade were helping the 101st Airborne in Operation Benton, other units of the 196th launched a separate, nameless operation along the northernmost five kilometres of coastline in Quang Ngai Province. Because American troops had been fired on almost every time they entered this coastal area, the 196th Light Brigade had decided that the best course of action would be to evacuate its inhabitants, who were thought to number five thousand; to destroy their villages; and to convert the area into a free-strike zone. The first stage of the operation was planned for the morning of August 21st, when elements of the 196th would make a surprise landing in amphibious tractors (usually called Amtracs) at Tuyet

Diem, a fishing village on a small peninsula. During the next three hours, the population of the village, estimated at six hundred, would dismantle their houses and take the beams and roof thatching, and also all their possessions and animals, down to the beach and aboard two landing craft that were to be brought near the shore in front of the village. Then, according to the plan, the landing craft—making as many trips as necessary—would sail down the coast to a lot that had been cleared in preparation for the operation, and the villagers would set up their village in the new spot. The newly cleared lot had formerly been the site of a large village called Son Tra, which had been shelled by the Marines about two years before. At that time, its people had been evacuated to a roadside a few kilometres away, where they erected huts to live in. A week before the operation that was to destroy Tuyet Diem was launched, the Army arranged to employ the villagers of Son Tra to level the ruins of their old village in preparation for the arrival of the villagers of Tuyet Diem. The villagers of Son Tra were given hints that they were clearing their old village in preparation for their own return. By conveying these hints, the Army hoped to prevent the National Liberation Front from guessing that the site was being cleared in preparation for a new military operation. The Americans who planned the evacuation of Tuyet Diem and the other coastal villages were much gratified by the neatness and simplicity of their plan, especially when they compared it with other evacuation projects that had been carried out in the province. As they saw it, the evacuation would not create "refugees" of the kind that had proved such a burden in the government camps. One colonel said of it, "We're just going to interrupt the villagers' work for six hours. They're not going to lose their chance to work, like the other refugees we've got. They can just bring their boats down the coast and start right up again with the new village. The real beauty of this is that all we have to supply is one day's food. They're going to bring their houses right along with them, so we won't need to bring any extra supplies for houses. This isn't going to be like those operations where five thousand people come into a camp with nothing to eat and nowhere to stay. This is going to be the best Civil Affairs operation we've run yet. The refugee people have been preparing for it for a full week." Mr. Ernest Hobson was far from happy about any operation that would increase the number of displaced people in the province, but, he, too, said that the evacuation of Tuyet Diem was much the most carefully planned operation of the sort so far.

The American planners were particularly pleased with the arrival of a three-man Vietnamese Cultural Drama Team—a troupe of actors organized by the South Vietnamese government and sent on tour throughout the country—which would perform for the villagers during their first evening at the new site. The evening before the evacuation, the Cultural Drama Team performed for an audience of about a hundred G.I.s in an open movie theatre at one of the base camps of the 196th Light Brigade. Standing under floodlights on a low stage, two youths dressed in the black garments of farmers sang several rock-and-roll songs in Vietnamese, accompanying themselves on electric guitars. They then switched to Vietnamese songs for a time, and wound up with "When the Saints Go Marching In," which they sang in English, in high, reedy voices. The second half of the performance was a magic show. Whereas the singers had remained perfectly deadpan throughout their concert, the magician, who couldn't have been more than eighteen, never once relaxed a wide, tense smile as he moved through his routine, and he moved through it as though every step and every flourish of his hands had been mapped out in advance. Among other tricks, he made a glass of water disappear; folded up a dollar bill in a piece of paper, burned the paper, and pulled the bill, intact, from the ashes; made three scarves tie themselves together in midair; and produced a bouquet of paper flowers from his assistant's ear. At the beginning of the magic show, the G.I.s clapped politely, but their interest soon waned, and then, the audience having suddenly been attacked by a swarm of large, bumbling insects that resembled fat dragonflies, the magician lost its attention completely. After the show, a colonel who was involved in the planning of the evacuation made a sour face and said to a fellow-officer, "Are *they* going to play tomorrow night? I don't think *I'd* want to watch them if *I'd* just been moved out of *my* village."

The next morning, I accompanied the soldiers of the 196th Light Brigade that landed in Tuyet Diem. The troops assembled at four-thirty at the top of a gently rising field in front of the base camp, and at five o'clock the men started walking down a dirt road to the beach in two single lines, each man keeping ten yards between himself and the man in front of him. A three-quarter moon faintly illumined the road from behind a high cover of thin, milky clouds. A deep thumping of artillery shells landing in rapid series, which had begun at about one o'clock, continued well into the morning at a stepped-up pace, and to the east, over the peninsula where the troops were to land, the sky periodically flashed a dull yellow. The morning was warm and muggy, and the troops, in their battle gear, began to sweat freely. The double column descended from the high ground in front of the camp and approached the clusters of tiny huts that the villagers of Son Tra had built themselves. Single candles burned in several huts as people rose for the day. A low sound of talking in the houses ceased as our presence became known; a dog barked and was silenced with a sharp word. A small girl stood in a low doorway and watched the troops pass, and a woman at a well paused with her hands on the well rope. An old man stood naked in a small dirt yard in the dim moonlight. When the troops had been walking for fifteen or twenty minutes, a single line of ARVN soldiers passed wordlessly between the two American lines, heading in the opposite direction. A rooster crowed, although dawn had not yet broken. The column halted.

Abruptly, someone called out, "Where the fuck are we?" The voice was shockingly loud in the silence of the dark road.

"Ah, shit, we're lost," someone else said angrily.

An officer walked up to the head of the column, and after a minute the column started to move again. The two lines, observed by four silent young Vietnamese men who were squatting in a row on a stone wall, passed through a wooden gate onto the beach. An elderly fisherman in black stood motionless by his boat, smoking a cigarette, as the soldiers filed past him. Apparently, the leaders had taken a wrong path, for, after another halt, they led the column through a brambly field to the road they had just left. Ten minutes later, the soldiers arrived on the beach again, at a point where two Amtracs were waiting on the sand. The men had a brief rest, and most of them got out cigarettes and began smoking. When the order came, they climbed eight-foot ladders running up the sides of the Amtracs, and sat down on their metal decks.

In one Amtrac, a platoon sergeant grumbled loudly as the men were seating themselves, "Everyone around here is a goddam Yankee. All Ah see is goddam Yankees every-where Ah go." To a G.I. near him he said, "You're a Yankee, aren't you, soldier?"

The soldier did not answer.

"Ah ain't no Yankee, Sarge," another soldier said.

Presently, the ponderous, box-shaped Amtracs rolled off the beach into the water. The point of departure was just inside the mouth of the Song Tra Bong river, and the square-bowed Amtracs had to buck a heavy incoming tide to get out to sea. Then, after a twenty-minute voyage across calm water, we came in sight of Tuyet Diem. It was almost full daylight. From the water, only ten or twelve of the houses in the village could be seen. As the invasion force approached, a woman on a front porch who was gathering something into her arms went on with her task, and a man standing up to his knees in the water next to a fishing boat and working with its rigging kept on doing so, and glanced up only briefly, as though the arrival at Tuyet Diem of two Amtracs bearing American soldiers were an everyday occurrence. The Amtracs rolled up on the beach, and the soldiers jumped quickly to the sand, a few of them falling over backward under the weight of their ammunition belts, heavy packs, and weapons. One squad walked quickly up a rough pasture, with their M-16s in firing position at their hips. Another filed north along the beach. Rounding a rocky promontory, the men of this squad arrived at the edge of the village, which fronted on a crescent of white sand and was protected at each end by several giant gray boulders—some as large as two-story houses—extending into the sea. At the north end of the cove, a stony island no more than fifty feet across, which was topped with a stand of straggling pine trees, helped provide a lee for the beach. Out at sea, a fleet of half a dozen fishing boats under full sail was visible on the horizon. (These fishing boats drew only two feet of water, were about six feet wide and thirty feet long, had long, heavy bowsprits, and sailed under a gaff rig.) Facing the water were half a dozen stone houses of two or three rooms. Some had porches whose roofs were supported by gaily painted stone pillars. The walls of these houses were decorated with molding, and the cornices, windowsills, and door frames were painted with patterns in bright blues, reds, oranges, and greens. Palm trees and bamboos arched above the houses, casting a mottled shade.

Several families stood watching silently as the troops filed into the village. The soldiers, too, were silent. Each of the Vietnamese, male or female, wore a simple black collarless garment with three-quarter-length trousers. Each of the women and the little girls wore her hair long down her back, held in place with a silver oval clasp. Most of the villagers had bare feet, and children under three wore no pants. A few soldiers poked their heads briefly in at doorways, but most of them simply walked along the pathways between the houses, intently scanning the scene around them as they proceeded; they were on the lookout for signs of the enemy. Only the sergeant who had been complaining about Yankees on the Amtrac was more aggressive in his search. He walked directly up to a neatly-groomed, wiry middle-aged man who, with his wife and son, was standing in front of one of the most prosperous-looking houses, and, pointing inside, demanded, "What's in here?" Getting no answer, he went inside, pointed to a large ornate chest, and said, "Open this."

The Vietnamese man looked at him questioningly.

"*Dammit, Ah said open this!*" the sergeant shouted, striking the chest with his gun butt.

The man opened it, revealing a pile of folded clothes.

187

The sergeant poked inside with the barrel of his gun and then left.

Outside again, the sergeant demanded, "Where V.C.? *Beaucoup* V.C., hunh?" (*"Beaucoup"* is a standard word in G.I. pidgin Vietnamese.) No one replied. As he passed another house, he noticed that the shutters on a side window were wired closed, and he bashed at them with his gun butt, but they did not break open, and he continued on his way without bothering to enter the house, whose front door stood ajar.

A few moments later, the sergeant pushed aside a curtain over the front entrance to a third house, and found himself facing an old man who was sitting on the floor just inside, bobbing his head and saying something that sounded like "Ow-ow-ow-ow-ow."

"Ow-ow-ow-ow-ow," mimicked the sergeant. "You're fuckin' crazy, that's what. Ow-ow-ow-ow-ow."

A central path wound back through the village, which was spread out on a hill. Directly behind one of the shore-front houses, a pile of rubble lay on a house foundation, and a palm tree about ten inches thick had been snapped in two halfway up, so that its leafy head—still green—was bowed into a neighbor's yard. "Artillery," a soldier remarked when he came upon the scene. Farther up the hill, the houses were poorer and were crowded closer together. Most had one or two rooms, were built of clay packed into woven bamboo frames, and were roofed with thatch. At the crest of the hill, the landscape opened out onto about two acres of flat rice fields. The troops who had headed up through the pasture when they debarked from the Amtracs were sitting on a steep, sandy hill that rose immediately behind the rice fields and gave them a view of the entire village. A dozen houses that were as large and well made as those on the shore surrounded the fields. Two other houses bordering the fields were in ruins. Recent artillery fire had made several big craters in a young crop of rice, and had sprayed mud over what remained of the rice shoots and onto the grassy embankments dividing the fields. The central path that led up the hill from the sea ran along its crest, parallel to the shore, for a few hundred yards, and then descended the hill to the shore farther north, at a place where treeless dunes covered with beach grass swept back from a long white beach.

Half an hour after the troops arrived, a Psychological Warfare Team consisting of an American and a Vietnamese began making announcements with a tape recorder and a loudspeaker. They announced that American troops had arrived to free the villagers from Vietcong domination, and ordered them to dismantle their houses and load the building materials, their possessions, and their animals on the landing craft (which had not yet arrived) within the next three hours. They also announced that the soldiers would help the people carry their possessions down to the boats. The commanding officer did not issue an order to this effect to his soldiers but allowed each man to decide for himself whether he would carry anything. The two landing craft arrived shortly after the announcements, one pulling up in the cove in front of the center of the village and the other at the long stretch of sand to the north. The villagers began to work as soon as they understood the nature of the situation. American troops that had entered other villages in Quang Ngai had usually found few able men, but at Tuyet Diem they found that a third of the families had men at home. Everyone, from the very old down to children of five or six, began carrying bundles to the beach. The villagers kept their stores of rice in waist-high pottery jars, and these were the most difficult objects to carry. Little girls and old women who were not accompanied by men importuned the American soldiers for help by tugging at their sleeves and attempting to pull them along to their houses. Four or five soldiers consented to help, and at once three or four little girls and a few old women gathered around them and tugged at their sleeves, trying to pull them in different directions, and smiling coaxingly or making sad faces. Neither the young men nor the young women ever smiled or asked for help. Most of the villagers set about carrying their belongings down the hill with a cold, fierce determination. Working against the three-hour deadline, they balanced huge loads at the ends of bamboo poles and made for the beach at a rapid, smooth, dancing jog. One old woman wept freely and loudly as she walked down the hill with a load. Other women wept soundlessly. One young woman's eyes streamed, even though her features were tightly composed, as she bent her energies to the work. All the children over five or six worked silently and hard, without any urging from their parents. Children of nine or ten carried two- and three-year-old brothers and sisters to the beach, leaving the heavier burdens of food, cooking utensils, and furniture to their parents. On the long open beach, the smallest children stood crying in groups of two and three next to their families' furniture and bundles of belongings. The four or five Americans who had taken up shoulder poles smiled and winked at one another with embarrassment as they passed on the path, in the manner of adults who have good-naturedly consented to take part in a children's game. To most of the soldiers, the villagers' possessions looked hardly worth carrying anywhere. Besides their jars of rice, the villagers wished to bring down large jars of *nuoc mam*—a major food staple for them, made of fermented fish, which gives off an odor that is usually disagreeable to Americans smelling it for the first time. They also carried bundles of twigs and reeds for firewood. When one American soldier was asked whether he intended to carry any of the villagers' belongings to the boats, he looked around him at the bundles on the beach and said, "What? *Me* carry *this shit?*" The villagers were wiry and strong, and even the women carried loads sufficient to tax a young G.I. (When a G.I. relieved one old woman of two bundles of firewood, he lifted them to his shoulder, and then set them down again and handed one to another soldier to carry and, looking at the frail old woman, put on an expression of amazement for the benefit of the other soldiers.) The combat soldiers in Vietnam are unusually big men, even by American standards, and at Tuyet Diem they loomed over most of the village men by more than a head. Some of the village women, apparently equating size with strength, led American soldiers to absurdly heavy loads and motioned to them to carry these to the beach. One old woman led an American at a half run to her hut, where she began desperately digging with her hands into the packed sandy earth of its floor. At length, she uncovered two huge jars of rice, each weighing about a hundred and fifty pounds. She secured one jar to each end of a shoulder pole with a wire hook and motioned impatiently to the American to take them away. Later, he and a man from the village together carried a jar at a time, with difficulty, down the path, one of them at each end of a shoulder pole.

Around eleven o'clock, the sun began to burn through the clouds, and the Americans who had been carrying belongings sat down and stopped work for the day, almost overcome by the heat. At eleven-fifteen, a sudden burst of machine-gun fire sent up a line of small geysers in the cove, about fifty feet from the shore. The commanding officer sent a patrol out along the beach, but the source of the fire was never ascertained. These were the only shots fired that day. (The Tuyet Diem operation was unusual in its lack of contact with the enemy. The military can almost never predict when the enemy will choose to resist in force, but most operations encounter sniper fire, at least, or small-unit fighting that results in both American and enemy casualties.)

The landing craft had been able to pull up to within ten yards of the shore, where the water was waist-deep. Each time a landing craft departed, many of the villagers, believing that the last boatload of belongings was leaving, waded deep into the water with bundles in their arms, and the soldiers on board shouted at them, "No more! That's all!," and attempted to prevent them from pushing their bundles onto the lip of the craft. Once, as a landing craft pulled away from the shore, a man ignored the protests of a soldier who stood at the rear of the craft, and, wading out up to his shoulders, tried repeatedly to shove a bundle of cooking utensils aboard. The soldier, becoming angry, pushed the man's bundle into the water. Some two dozen ARVN troops arrived late in the morning on one of the landing craft. They did not carry anything to the beach. One of them had brought a transistor radio, and a group of Americans persuaded him to tune it to the American armed-forces radio network. Light music, of the kind usually heard in restaurants or elevators in the United States, issued across the crowded beach. Another group of American soldiers sat on a poncho eating combat rations and drinking the milk of coconuts they had taken from nearby trees. Several soldiers had brought cameras, and they took pictures of the villagers carrying loads to the beach, and also of the landing craft jammed with firewood, furniture, bundles, jars of food, hobbled animals, and villagers. (The military in Vietnam apparently encourage the men to take snapshots of the war to send home. In the photographic department of the Danang PX, there hung a poster showing a picture of houses and palm trees silhouetted against a conflagration that filled most of the poster with red-and-orange flame and black smoke. In the foreground was a larger-than-life-size profile, in black silhouette, of the helmeted head of a G.I.; he was holding a camera to his eye and pressing the shutter. A caption at the bottom read, "SEND HOME A PHOTOGRAPHIC HISTORY OF THE WAR IN VIETNAM.")

To get their belongings from the beach to the landing craft, some villagers made use of large, shallow baskets woven of reeds and waterproofed with a coating of tar or resin. (The fishing villages along the coast in Quang Ngai use baskets of this type as small boats. It was in these simple craft that the villagers had first launched out on the water as children; in front of other coastal villages I often saw the water dotted with children in baskets, who propelled themselves about at a surprising speed with a sculling stroke of a single paddle.) During the morning, men who had been out in their fishing boats returned to Tuyet Diem, and helped carry belongings to the landing craft. By noon, it was apparent that the population of the village was not six hundred, as had been thought, but about fifteen hundred, so the deadline for the dismantling of the village was extended until late afternoon.

At Son Tra, where the villagers were being landed after their journey down the coast, a team of American soldiers had been detailed to help them carry their possessions ashore. Around the newly cleared lot that was to be the villagers' new home, a barbed-wire fence had been erected to insure that everyone checked in through a registration tent, for fingerprinting and questioning, and through a Red Cross tent, for a brief medical checkup.

Perhaps because the number of people so far exceeded expectations, rendering the medical and security facilities inadequate for even the most cursory checking, someone had cut a large breach in the fence, and several hundred villagers had poured through to claim spots on the lot. On the lot, three stone buildings, including a roofless church, remained standing. Children's line drawings of helicopters, cattle, pigs, and gunboats had been scratched into the paint on the inside walls of one building. At one end of the lot was a little rocky hill that had been reduced to a blackened knob dotted with shattered stumps of trees during the Marines' bombing and shelling about two years before. Because of the delay in the schedule, American officers at Son Tra decided to postpone the destruction of the village of Tuyet Diem until the next day, and to blow up only the wells that night, to keep the Vietcong from getting water there. The officer detailed to the task said that because they were good, deep wells, with stone shafts part way down, he would need several hundred pounds of explosives to destroy them all.

An ARVN sergeant had been appointed "village chief," to control and organize the Tuyet Diem villagers at their new site. The Americans present always referred to him by his new title and spoke to him with the same humble deference that I had seen accorded to Lieutenant Colonel Tho in Quang Tin. The village chief was a tall, thin young man with a tight-lipped, impatient air, who wore a freshly pressed khaki uniform, stiff and glistening with starch, and French-style glasses with rims of clear plastic that extended only across the top of the lenses. At about two o'clock, when I arrived at the beach in front of the lot, he was in a state of fury because the gap in the barbed-wire fence had rendered the registration procedure meaningless. He paced up and down just inside the barbed-wire fence shouting through an electric bullhorn, telling the villagers they should remain on the beach, but his order came much too late; about half the new arrivals had already entered the empty lot. At one point, nine middle-aged and elderly men approached him, with their conical straw hats in their hands, and a spokesman for the group told him that the villagers were afraid the Vietcong would come to Son Tra to kill them in the night, because they had not resisted evacuation from their homes in Tuyet Diem. The newly appointed village chief interrupted the spokesman in mid-sentence and, shaking with anger, shouted that he would listen to no demands of any kind at that moment, because no one was supposed to have even come through to his side of the fence yet. The spokesman started to say something more, and the village chief rushed at him and, in swift succession, struck him on the face with the front and then the back of his hand and kicked him on the hip. The spokesman fell back as he was beaten, and said nothing more. Several American officers were sitting nearby in a jeep talking, and one of them—an adviser to the new village chief—remarked to me, "Looks like they're having a little row." At my request, he went over to the chief with his interpreter to ask what had happened, and after returning and explaining the situation to me he observed, "The village chief believes that you have to be tough at first to gain their respect in order to control them."

Because the villagers had had neither the time nor the manpower to dismantle their houses and load the materials on the landing craft, as the Army had originally planned, and no building supplies had been made available, the villagers slept for the next few weeks under pieces of cloth propped up on sticks, or under their tarred basket boats. During that time, they began constructing makeshift dwellings of poles that they cut for themselves in a patch of woods nearby. The first night, they camped here and there all over the lot, but the next day they learned that theirs was only the first of a number of villages to be moved into the enclosure, and they were made to squeeze into one corner at the back. That day, the village chief performed his first administrative act, which was to take everyone's identification card away, so that no one could leave the enclosure. The same day, the Army decided to evacuate another village right away, and consequently a thousand more people arrived on the lot, bringing the official estimate of its population up to twenty-five hundred. Even then, only half the lot could be used, for more villages were scheduled for evacuation in the near future. Later that week, troops of the 196th Light Brigade blew up and then burned the empty village of Tuyet Diem. The Army put off the evacuation and destruction of the other villages until after the Presidential election, on September 3rd, because the troops of the 196th were needed to provide security around the polls.

Like most of the American military in Vietnam, the Army men who evacuated the villagers from Tuyet Diem and then destroyed the village saw what they were doing as only the first stage of a long-range benevolent plan for all of South Vietnam, in which the country would be rebuilt and then would develop a free and democratic government. This first stage of the plan—the destruction of the villages—usually went very smoothly, and gave rise to considerable optimism among the Americans who carried it out, but the second stage—the stage in which the Vietnamese and their American civil-affairs advisers were to rebuild and reorganize villages like Tuyet Diem, and were to stitch the whole society back together again—turned out to be infinitely more difficult than anyone had expected, and the people who were to carry it out could not even

begin to match the scale of destruction with their construction. More often than not, the reality of the villagers' new
life under the South Vietnamese government turned out
to be a crowded tent in a government camp or a bare lot
like the one in Son Tra. Many optimistic Americans,
including reporters as well as military men and civilian
officials, tended to set off the destruction caused by the
military effort against the construction resulting from the
civil-affairs effort, seeing the two results as separate but
balanced "sides" of the war; and, looking at our commit-
ment of men and materials, they were often favorably
impressed with the size of the constructive effort, almost as
though it were being carried out in one country while the
military effort was being carried out in another. But, of
course, the two programs were being carried out in the
same provinces and the same villages, and the people who
received the allotments of rice were the same people whose
villages had been destroyed by bombs. The Vietnamese
civilians felt the effects of the two programs not as two
abstract "sides" of the war but as a continuing experience
in the single reality of their daily lives, and, from their
point of view, the aid given them by the Americans and
the South Vietnamese government amounted to only a
tiny measure of compensation (although extravagant
promises were made in the leaflets and in other propaganda) for enormous losses and suffering. Many Americans, both civilian and military, tended not to see beyond
the particular program they were involved in. Civil-affairs
officials, forgetting that it was American firepower that had
been the original direct cause of the destitution of the vast
majority of the people in the camps, were puzzled when
these hungry, tired people showed little gratitude for the
help that the Americans and the G.V.N. were giving them.
Many of the civil-affairs officials were working exhaust-

ingly long hours and doing the best job they could with their limited time and resources, and they could not see why the people should complain and expect more than they were getting. Many military men, for their part, were loyal only to *their* duty—that of conducting military operations. Having efficiently carried out the "military half," they saw it as the responsibility of the Vietnamese government and of the American civil-affairs advisers to carry out the "civilian half" by taking care of the people who had been hurt or dispossessed in the "military half." (Thus, although, in the two weeks of Operation Benton, Task Force Oregon destroyed about sixty-five per cent of the houses of an estimated seventeen thousand people, the officer in charge of the 101st's Civil Affairs Office had been able to answer my question about the future of the area's population by saying, *"We* don't have any plans for the immediate future. It's the responsibility of the G.V.N. and the ARVN to carry out Pacification and Revolutionary Development." He did not know that the G.V.N. had no plan for these people.) But because, along with the destruction of villages, American military operations brought death to many civilians, American civil-affairs workers, no matter how well intentioned they might be, and no matter how well supplied they might someday become, could never, from the point of view of the villagers, "balance" the sufferings caused by the military, or undo what they had done, which was often absolute and irreversible.

On August 30th, in a wing of the province chief's office in Quang Ngai City, I was granted an interview with Mr. James A. May, a civilian, who was the Senior Adviser for Quang Ngai Province. Mr.

May, who is from California, is forty-seven years old, stands several inches over six feet, and has a long, bushy mustache. On the job in Quang Ngai, he often wore a Mexican sombrero and Western-style leather boots. Mr. May is a voluble talker, and when I asked for his view of the condition of the Pacification Program in Quang Ngai, on which he is the chief adviser, he warmed to the subject quickly, and delivered an impromptu talk that began with a description of the activities of the Marines. "The Marines came in May of 1965," he said. "Task Force Oregon came into a situation where, although the friendlies had made progress for two years, it was only moderate progress. There was quite a bit of forward and back, but, on balance, we nibbled ahead. The problem was that Charlie had occupied large portions of the province since the Japs. As far as Charlie was concerned, until the Marines arrived he had hardly been touched by the war. In many areas, it was easy for him to believe he was winning, and the people were illiterate, so they didn't know what was happening. When the Marines came, the friendly operations could go into an area, but they'd retreat soon, so it was easy for Charlie to say, 'We ran them out.' But since Task Force Oregon arrived, there have been a number of changes that have been very visible to Charlie. Task Force Oregon has had three big advantages over the Marines. First, they have had the manpower to do the job. Second, they have had the firepower, which is also very important, for shock effect. Third, they have had more mobility, with their helicopters. The main thing they've been able to do is to drive Charlie out of his strongholds, keeping a kill ratio of ten to one. They have kept Charlie on the run. Their reaction speed and firepower were unbelievable. Charlie started out by following his usual pattern of shooting down choppers, but this time five more would come along and go after him. And the artillery was always there, and we could throw in an armored unit with tremendous speed. Charlie got everything *and* the kitchen sink thrown at him so hard that he didn't know what hit him. Before Task Force Oregon came, Mo Duc and Duc Pho"—two districts in the south of Quang Ngai Province—"were Charlie's. But now he's had so many casualties that he's had to revise all his plans. One big thing we've done is to repair Route 1 for transportation. Now Charlie can still snipe and harass, but he cannot effectively overrun a large village or overrun an outpost. Now he's all off balance. He's got communication problems, and his food supply and labor force are drying up. Aside from what he brings in on infiltration routes, he's had a tough time."

I asked Mr. May if he meant that by destroying the villages the Army had deprived the Vietcong of their use.

"In a few areas, the villages have been destroyed," Mr. May said, "This is a necessary side effect if you're going to fight hard. We've invited the people to come on out of the V.C. villages to secure areas where it's safe. The V.C. use villages as protection, the way a gangster uses a hostage. So in the process of getting at Charlie it's inevitable that the village gets it. You'll notice that the undestroyed areas are the ones that have not seen a G.V.N.-and-Allied Forces-versus-V.C. confrontation. That's the way war is. To me, it's just like the Second World War in places in France and Italy, where the villages were wiped out as far as you could see. You just can't get at the enemy unless you get at them where they're at. There isn't any way to get them but level the villages they are located in. You know, some of these villages have never known any kind of government other than the V.C. But we give them an opportunity to get out and go. Also, these mud houses with thatched roofs can be built up overnight. You send some people back into an area, and in a week the place is all built up again. So I expect to see a lot more destruction. But the destruction works both ways. Just two weeks ago, the V.C. attacked a village on Route 1 in Son Tinh District that was protected by the Popular Forces, and blew up about twenty houses, with a lot of civilian casualties. Gradually, we're depriving the V.C. of his labor force and food. Now we've got about fifty thousand people in camps and about seventy-five thousand people who have built their own houses or are living with friends. Little by little, the people are realizing that security lies in the secure zones. They're beginning to see that the business opportunities are here in the cities, and they're coming in by the thousand now."

I asked about the operation I had just seen carried out in the village of Tuyet Diem.

"Well, technically they are not counted as refugees, because they were resettled right there," Mr. May said. "They brought the parts of their houses down and can set them up again. It's amazing with these Vietnamese houses. They can take them down and then put them right back up again, like an Erector set."

I asked him how the Pacification of villages was proceeding.

To answer this, Mr. May pulled out of his desk a map of the province as big as an unfolded newspaper. Along Route 1 and around the town of Duc Pho, the map was washed over in light blue. In the northern part of the province, the blue area along Route 1 was from one to five kilometres wide. "This shows the pacified areas when the Marines got here in 1965," he said. "We could hardly go outside Quang Ngai City. Now the area is much bigger." With one finger he delineated a blue area that bulged out about ten kilometres from the road in Son Tinh District and around Quang Ngai City.

Then Mr. May took me into a conference room down a

hall, where a much larger map hung on the wall. It was dotted with black-headed pins, which indicated the presence of Revolutionary Development Teams—groups of young Vietnamese men sent out to win rural people over to the Saigon government's side. "We've got forty-seven Revolutionary Development Teams," he told me.

Looking at the map, I saw that all but three or four of them were stationed along Route 1 or in the undestroyed region around Quang Ngai City.

"The R.D. Program has proved itself many times over by now," he said. "We have plans to expand Pacification considerably. Even in the worst days, it has been successful. The program has grown steadily."

I asked him what, in his view, it meant to say that a village was "pacified" or had been made "secure."

"Well, it means that it's highly improbable that the V.C. would dare infiltrate into it in the daytime," Mr. May said. "Of course, this is hard to determine, because sometimes the V.C. run out of no place, like Indians attacking a fort on the frontier at night."

I mentioned that in Son Tinh District, where a large number of Revolutionary Development Teams were working along Route 1, an American lieutenant colonel had advised an observer from Saigon against sleeping in any village in the province.

"I heard about that, and I jumped the colonel on that," Mr. May said. "I mean, for an American to be able to sleep in a village would be a very special situation, quite different from a regular Vietnamese sleeping there. It would be more like a village chief trying to sleep in the village. The village is secure for most Vietnamese, but the village chief can't sleep there, because the V.C. have got it in for him in particular. So I'd say that's not a very good measurement. You might say that a pacified area is an area that is more secure than before but not yet completely secure. The villages are not perfect everywhere. What the V.C. have to face is: How much will they pay for a victory? Will they lose more than they gain if they take a city? For instance, the V.C. might be able to come right into the province capital—I'm not saying they couldn't—but it's a question of how much it would cost them."

I asked Mr. May whether he considered the physical destruction of villages in wide areas of the province an impediment to the Pacification Program.

"I don't think it makes a tremendous amount of difference," he replied. "Once we provide security for an area, the people flock right back out and build the place up themselves again in no time. For instance, Charlie took over one village in '64, and we ran him out in '65, and the village got pretty damaged, but when we designated the place a secure area, the people came flocking back by the thousand. Then Charlie overran it again and the people left again. Then, when we took it again, the people came right back again. Then Charlie took the place again, and this time some of the people stayed there, but the point is that if we secure an area the people will come right back in again and build the place right up again in no time. Soon we plan to provide real and lasting security for that village. We keep a record of how the Pacification of each village is going. It's a document with a lot of questions on it, and we feed all the questions into a computer."

Later, I saw a Pacification "point sheet" that had been used by the Marines. It, too, was of a standardized type. The record for one village was as shown on the following facing pages.

High officials who received standardized reports like this one talked of the G.V.N.'s Pacification Program only in terms of progress, trying to judge whether the progress was slow or fast, and when one program (such as the G.V.N.'s Strategic Hamlet Program) failed, and a new, improved

	OBJECTIVE	MAX POINTS	POINTS
I.	*Destruction of Organized V.C. Military Forces*		
	A. V.C. local/main force units destroyed or driven out	15	6
	B. G.V.N. forces capable of defending area	5	2
	Total	20	8
II.	*Destruction of V.C. Infrastructure*		
	A. Census completed	2	1
	B. V.C. infrastructure discovered, destroyed, or neutralized	8	2
	C. G.V.N. intelligence network established	5	1
	D. Census Grievance Teams completed interviewing each family	2	1
	E. Principal grievance completely processed	3	1
	Total	20	6
III.	*Establishment of Local Security*		
	A. Defense plans completed	2	1
	B. Defense construction completed	3	2
	C. Permanent local defense forces trained and in place	12	5
	D. Communications established with military supporting unit	3	3
	Total	20	11
IV.	*Establishment of Local Government*		
	A. Village chief and council appointed and functioning	2	2
	B. Village chief and council elected	2	0
	C. Village chief lives in village and is able to sleep there	3	3
	D. Hamlet chief's appointed councils functioning	2	0

OBJECTIVE	MAX POINTS	POINTS
E. Hamlet chiefs, councils elected	4	0
F. Hamlet chiefs live in hamlets and are able to sleep there	4	1
G. Permanent Psy Ops and Public Information services established	1	1
H. Village statutes enacted	1	0
I. Social and administrative organization of villages completed to meet immediate needs of villagers	1	0
Total	20	7

V. *Completion of Initial New Life Programs*

	MAX POINTS	POINTS
A. Public health	4	2
B. Education	4	3
C. Agricultural	4	3
D. Markets	4	3
E. Transportation	4	2
Total	20	13
Final Total	100	45

program (such as the G.V.N.'s New Life Hamlet Program) was instituted in its place, they always spoke in terms of the G.V.N.'s having a chance to make a fresh start at "winning the hearts and minds of the people," as though the earlier failures had had no effect on the countryside and the situation in 1967 were the same as the situation in 1964 or 1965. But at the lower level, in provinces like Quang Ngai, American civil-affairs officials and workers faced a situation in which the cumulative effect of the many abortive programs—all of them accompanied, from 1965 on, by the full force of the Americans' overwhelming firepower—had been to bring disruption, destruction, and death to the countryside on an immense scale and to leave among the people an indelible bitterness that no new program—unless it were a program to raise the dead—could hope to overcome. Before American civil-affairs workers in Quang Ngai became optimistic about any new programs for the G.V.N., they had to ask themselves whether the G.V.N. had any presence whatever in most of the villages, and, what was more to the point, whether there were many villages left in Quang Ngai in which anyone could have a presence.

I asked Mr. May about the official policy toward the people who continued to live in the zones of harassment-and-interdiction artillery fire.

"These people have had a choice," Mr. May said. "They still think Charlie's going to win. We've plastered the place with Chieu Hoi leaflets. And when we bring them into secured areas we try to get them to stay, but the pull of the land is very strong. But all the people have to do to keep their village from being destroyed is make sure that their hamlet isn't a fort for Charlie. But, for instance, down in Duc Pho they're not even trying, because Charlie *is* their government right now. Still, we've been encouraged by the number of people who have come to live along the highway, and also by the number who have started living on the beaches. We know they're not dangerous out there, because they haven't got any cover, and they can't dig underground so well there."

I asked if he thought it was a good idea to hold all the villagers responsible when the Vietcong chose to fire at our troops from their village.

"If you let him in your village, you're an accomplice, aren't you?" Mr. May said. "If you're feeding him and working for him, aren't you an accomplice?"

I asked about conditions in the camps.

"There's always plenty to eat, and a roof over their head," Mr. May said. "It does get a little overcrowded. It's not like a first-class hotel, with someone giving you a big welcome. I don't maintain that the refugee performance is like that. But we give them a free choice about whether to come or not. Usually, some want to come and some don't. Some people look and see that everyone else is getting aboard a chopper, so they get aboard, too. And when they go back, sometimes someone just says, 'There's been no fightin' in the village, so let's go back.' But we don't encourage them to go back until their native area is completely liberated. Some people want to know, 'Aren't we going to create a nation of refugees living on the dole?' This has been proved totally without foundation. The refugees have a better standard of living than they did in their villages. Look at the tin on their roofs. It's better than the old thatched roofs—it doesn't leak. And the refugee camps bring the people in closer to the urban centers, where they can have modern experiences and learn modern practices. It's a modernizing experience. The peasant is ignorant, but he isn't stupid. He knows business opportunities when he sees them. But I'll say one thing: You never have any trouble getting them to go back to their villages!" He laughed. Summing matters up, he added, "This is a tough, new kind of war. It's kind of like the Indian wars. There's no fast and easy way to finish it. There are so many places for the V.C. to hide—just like the Indians did. But I'd expect this province to be pacified in three or four years. And if we can pacify Quang Ngai, we can pacify any province. In three or four years, we may not have wiped out all the Charlies, but we will have cut him off from the people and restricted him to the mountains, where he'll be nothing more than a nuisance, like tigers— not a serious threat. Already, Quang Ngai is a bustling beehive of activity. Things are going well. I decided two years ago that I didn't come out here to lose. But if I thought our practice or theory was wrong, I'd get out."

In October, I received a report on the subject of civilian war casualties from a British civilian physician who had been working in Quang Ngai for over three years. In the report, he said that as of October, 1967, the number of patients in the province's only civilian hospital was between five hundred and fifty and six hundred and fifty a day. Of these, about fifty per cent were surgical cases. For example, on October 6th, three hundred and five of five hundred and sixty patients were in the surgical wards. Since the arrival of Task Force Oregon, the average number of war casualties admitted to the hospital each day had been thirty, although there were sometimes only ten admissions and sometimes forty.

> They come by Lambretta, hammock, motor-cycle, bicycle, and about twenty per cent by helicopter [the doctor wrote]. The latter [helicopter] presents a great problem, as they bring patients from far away to us that should be going to a hospital closer by—for example, we have patients from Quang Tin Province. To get them back home is nearly impossible. Of our surgical patients, ninety-five per cent are war casualties. War casualties break down: 1. Cannon—fifty-five per cent (and higher). 2. Bullet—fifteen per cent. 3. Bomb—fifteen per cent. 4. Grenade—three per cent. 5. Mine —two per cent. 6. War burns—eight to ten per cent.

The report explained that war burns were caused by napalm, phosphorus, flamethrowers, and jettisoned gasoline tanks, and continued:

We frequently have patients admitted with blast syndrome from bombing (air displacement) or gas poisoning from tunnels. Ten per cent of the latter usually die in hospital. There are very few home burns—less than one in twenty. We also get cases that have been tortured by ARVN or security police. The following illustrates how many casualties arrive at the province hospital. When shelling occurs, there are those slightly wounded. They stay home, probably five in ten. Of the remaining five, two die at home or on the way to the hamlet aid station or village dispensary. The latter is staffed by a technician, midwife, etc. One is treated at the dispensary and kept till he is well. The other two are taken to the province hospital by the relatives. When the relatives acknowledge the seriousness of the situation, they may take him at once instead of going to the dispensary. This is true for coastal areas. From the other areas very few reach the hospital. Situations in which injury occurs: 1. Innocently at home, working, eating, or sleeping—being shelled or bombed not aware of impending danger. 2. Bunkers, infrequently. 3. Bullet wounds from ground troops caught in the crossfire, or deliberately inflicted by the military.

If the doctor's estimate of the ratio of the number of civilian casualties who reached the hospital to the number who did not was correct, this would mean that there had been about fifty thousand civilian war casualties a year in Quang Ngai since American troops first arrived.

On the night of my interview with Mr. May, the Vietcong overran Quang Ngai City. They freed twelve hundred prisoners from the province jail, blew up two gas stations that served American vehicles, and fired mortar shells into the American military advisory compound, causing thirteen casualties. I spent that night in one of several American compounds in the city, and in the evening, before the attack, I sat talking with Mr. Hobson, the American provincial adviser for refugees, and several doctors and nurses who worked at the province hospital and lived in the compound. Americans all over the city had been informed that there was a strong probability that the Vietcong would attack the city that night. Mr. Hobson, who had spent several years as a parole officer in the United States, passed out guns and taught the doctors how to use them, but he had little confidence that an effective resistance could be put up if the Vietcong chose to attack their compound. "I don't think they're going to attack here, but they can go anywhere they want," he said. "And if they want you, they can get you." The compound was always guarded by four or five ARVN soldiers. At night, these guards had been falling asleep on the job more often than not, and the Americans in the compound had devised a system whereby each American stayed awake for three hours a night, in rotating shifts, in order to keep the ARVN guards awake.

At about nine o'clock, an elderly Red Cross nurse with white hair and a prim, kindly face came into Mr. Hobson's part of the compound to ask his advice about what to do in the event of an attack.

Mr. Hobson advised her to lock herself and the nurses she shared quarters with in their room. Then he asked, "Do you want a gun?"

"Oh, my, no! I wouldn't know how to use a gun!" the elderly nurse replied, in a tone of mixed shock and amusement and delight.

"Well, then, shall I get you my knife?" Mr. Hobson asked, and his joke seemed to catch the mood of this group of reluctant soldiers, for everyone, including the nurse, burst out laughing.

At two o'clock, after most of the group had gone to bed in their rooms in the compound, heavy machine-gun fire sounded from the direction of the prison, which was perhaps two hundred yards down the road, and then came the thumping of incoming mortar shells. Everyone got out of bed and looked out into the darkness. Soon there was the sharp crack of artillery, followed by the faint whistle of the shells going overhead. Mr. Hobson explained that whenever the Vietcong attacked, artillery began to fire all over the countryside at "suspected enemy troop concentrations." The firing down the road continued for an hour and then subsided, and the people in the compound returned to bed.

In the morning, large crowds of the townspeople appeared on the streets and stood around in groups, talking. The city authorities had let the body of one youthful Vietcong, dressed only in a loincloth and sandals, lie in his blood on the street outside the liberated prison, as though to prove an ARVN and American victory. A Vietcong flag remained flying in a schoolyard until ten o'clock, however. When the schoolmaster was questioned by the authorities, he explained that he had been afraid to take the flag down by himself.

In the military advisory compound, several barracks had been damaged, and six jeeps in the central yard were immobilized, their tires punctured with mortar shrapnel. I found two officers surveying the scene.

"Do you think the girls'll come?" one officer asked the other.

"What girls?" the second officer asked.

"The *girls*," the first officer said. "The whores. On the picnic."

"Oh. I don't know. A lot of our Vietnamese workers in the offices don't show up after these attacks."

"Maybe some of the girls will show. Maybe I'll have to settle for No. 5 instead of the one I like—you know, No. 2."

I learned that one young American soldier had been killed as he ran in his pajamas from his barracks in the compound toward a bunker, and that twelve others had been wounded on their way to bunkers, or in their beds. No helicopters had been able to take off to suppress the enemy fire, because the mortar shells had landed right next to the helicopter pad from the first minute of the attack.

Later that day, I left for Saigon, and, by chance, I arrived there just in time to catch the last few minutes of a press conference that was being held by a high American official in the Pacification Program. He was speaking to an audience of over a hundred correspondents in an air-conditioned auditorium. Toward the end of the conference, a Japanese newsman asked him if there were any provinces that could be held up as models of progress in the Pacification Program. The official mentioned Binh Dinh Province, and added, "Another place where clear-and-hold has been proceeding remarkably well is in Quang Ngai. I think that Quang Ngai is going to turn out to be one of the success stories of 1967."

," a fac-
Birming-
ype was
of type
ision of